SVERRE SÆTRE

NORWEGIAN CAKES AND COOKIES

SVERRE SÆTRE

NORWEGIAN CAKES AND COOKIES

Scandinavian Sweets Made Simple

Coauthor: Hanne Hay Sætre
Translation by Kim Gardner
Photography by Christian Brun

Skyhorse Publishing

Contents

The New Norwegian Bakery

I have called what I work with "the new Norwegian bakery." That is because I am committed to making traditional Norwegian cakes and desserts, but with a new and original twist. This applies for example to desserts like veiled farm girls, compotes, and rice pudding, as well as classic baked goods like Kvæfjord (World's Best) cake, lefses (Norwegian griddle cakes), oatmeal macaroons, and sveler (Norwegian pancakes). These well-known and beloved recipes are favorites on many a Norwegian dinner table, but even though the original recipes are fantastic, I quite like the idea of bringing something new to them. For example, I do not avoid using both vanilla and saffron when I think these exotic flavors lift the classics yet another notch. At the same time, I am very committed to allowing the Norwegian flavor to come through. I also like to make use of modern techniques and often break a cake or dessert recipe down into its individual parts so as to put it together again in a new way. For example, waffles with blueberries and sour cream are transformed into sour cream and blueberry mousse sandwiches. This is how you get a delicious dessert with a completely new texture, but with the same beautiful, traditional flavors.

As a pastry chef, and especially as a member of the Norwegian National Culinary Team, I have managed to be part of a movement in recent years to promote Norwegian and Nordic raw materials. In the international culinary world, Norwegian raw materials have a high status. This especially applies to lamb, wild game, crayfish, and king crab. These raw materials have developed fantastic flavor and quality because of our harsh climate and our peculiar geographical relationship. If we look at the sweet kitchen—the borderline between bakery and dessert—we also have a large selection of good Norwegian raw materials. For example, fruit and berries—again, you can look at the harsh climate of Norway as beneficial. We cannot cultivate large quantities of them, but we get fruit and berries with exceptionally good flavors and qualities. Long, light summers with relatively low temperatures make it so that Norwegian fruit and berries take a long time to ripen, something that gives the flavors the opportunity to develop favorably over a much longer time than in warmer regions. When I, together with the Norwegian National Culinary Team, won the Culinary Olympics in 2008, we had Norwegian raw materials as the theme, and we let the Norwegian raw materials shine through in the desserts and in the chocolates we made. We used cloudberries, wild raspberries, rosehips, apples, and even porcini mushrooms in the chocolates, and they were a really big hit with the judges.

Other especially good Norwegian raw materials that I want to highlight in this book are our dairy products, which are also entirely world-class. When the Norwegian National Culinary Team travels around in the world and competes, we always have cream and butter from Norway with us. When it comes to butter, we use both dairy butter and Kviteseid butter. We also make great use of quark, sour cream, cream cheese, crème fraîche, and dense milk. In Norway, we also have some exciting ingredients that are less traditional. Examples of these are sea buckthorn and birch juice. These are good, but perhaps little known, raw materials that I explore in terms of potential and possibility in the new Norwegian bakery.

In my bakery, we use the raw materials of the seasons. We look forward to the rhubarb arriving in the spring, to the berry season of summer with strawberries and raspberries, and to the autumn when there is an abundance of locally produced fruit like apples and plums. We use all we can of fresh fruit and berries, as well as preserves and canned goods, so that we can serve canned plums, strawberry jelly, and jam throughout the winter. This gives us a great variety of goods to choose from in the course of a year, and the customers know what they can look forward to throughout the seasons.

It is my wish to preserve the pure and simple in the Norwegian raw materials while I innovate and surprise with new flavors and methods at the same time. It is about knowledge and creativity and other ways to use our fantastic raw materials, and most of all it is about entirely new and delicious taste experiences. Enjoy *Norwegian Cakes and Cookies*!

Sverre Sætre

www.sverresaetre.no

SVERRE SÆTRE
OSLO

Fruit

Crunchy, good apples, mild pears, sweet morellos . . . We don't have very many types of fruit in Norway, but those we do have are world-class. Our apples, plums, and morellos are in a class of their own when it comes to flavor. It is the long, light summer days and the relatively low temperature that makes the fruit ripen slowly here and develop a lot of extra flavor and sweetness. Unfortunately, the whole of our vast tract of land is not ideal for cultivating fruit, but parts of eastern and western Norway have proven to be perfect when it comes to climate and soil.

In Norway, we have preserved fruit with jamming, juicing, and canning since the old days. This is how you could use the fruit in food preparation beyond the fall and winter. Today, preserving has disappeared from the home for the most part and is used mostly by big industry, which seldom takes into account whether the raw materials are finished ripening before they're preserved. Moreover, so much sugar is poured on that they don't play a part. In my bakery, in terms of both health and nutrition, as well as taste, we have dusted off the good old art of refinement and can as much fruit as we can enjoy through the dark winter. If you treat the raw materials well and follow the recipe, you get canned goods of excellent quality. You should also know that if you wish to use the fruit whole, canning is actually a better storage method than freezing.

You probably do not immediately associate carrots and potatoes with baked goods, but I actually use a good deal of both of them in my bakery. Carrots and potatoes fit very well in cakes and desserts because they are mild in flavor and add a lot of moistness.

Apples

Crisp and juicy. This is what we associate with all of our varieties of apples, and in Norway we have some of the best apples in the world. Because the apple tree depends on cold resting periods in order to blossom, the growing conditions along the fjords of western Norway, and certain places in eastern Norway and as far north as North Trøndelag, are excellent for apple growing. Apples are used for almost everything, and they are ideal for further processing—for baking, frying, boiling, dehydrating, canning, pressing, wine making, and searing. In my bakery, we use apples in a lot of good things, like tarts and cakes; we cook them with vanilla; we make jellies, jam, and juice, veiled farm girls, chocolates, and apple chips, among others. Plus, we always make sure to use apples that are in season. Apples are perfect for gentle canning. After putting the apples in the jar, I usually add other good flavors, like lingonberries, cinnamon, and star anise, for example, in addition to a little sugar. When the apples are canned, completely new possibilities and applications emerge. Canned apples are very suitable as a filling for cream cakes, and also as a starting point for apple sorbet. Moreover, canned apples are the world's easiest—and quickest—dessert. If you have a jar of canned apples alone, the only thing you need to do is whip a little cream or make a vanilla sauce. A little sprinkle of crunchy, crisp rusks puts the finishing touch on it.

We divide the different apple varieties into three categories: summer apples, fall apples, and winter apples. The difference between them is how long they need to ripen, and how long the time of use is after harvesting.

Summer apples have a short time of use and ripen during August. They are often mild in flavor and have a low acid content. Some varieties are Close, July Red, Vista Bella, Transparente Blanche, Quinte, and Red Sävstadholm.

Fall apples get ripe during September. They tolerate a short shelf life of 1–2 months after harvesting. Some of our fall apple varieties are Prince, James Grieve, Summer Red, Gravenstein, and Åkerø. Winter apples do not finish ripening on the tree and therefore should be stored a few weeks before use. They are harvested during October and have a time of use of 3–4 months. Some winter apple varieties are Lobo, Ingrid Marie, Karin Schneider, Filippa, Aroma, and Torstein. There are good Norwegian apples on the market right up to January. It's good to know that these generally are not sprayed with pesticides. Each apple tree is, in fact, checked and sprayed only as needed.

Pears

Pears are both plump and juicy, but usually have no distinct flavor of their own. In exchange, the juiciness means that they fit perfectly in tarts and cakes, usually in combination with sour berries like lingonberries. Lingonberries add—besides their beautiful color—acidity that forms a nice counterbalance to the sweet pears and makes the flavor picture nuanced and exciting.

Common to all pears is that they have a short shelf life after harvesting. Therefore, they must either be consumed or refined fairly quickly. In order to preserve both flavor and texture in the best possible way, canning is a good method of conservation.

Since pears thrive best of all in dry and warm climates, Norway can never be a great pear country, but we have managed to get some varieties to thrive. The most common ones are Variegated July, Conference, Empress, Williams, Moltke, Anna, and Gray pears. My favorite variety is the Gray pear, which in addition to being sweet, juicy, and a little grainy, has a prominent spice flavor.

Plums

There is usually a delicate balance between

sweetness and acidity in Norwegian plums. It is this acidity that makes them so perfect in combination with dessert creams like vanilla mousse or lightly whipped cream. Plums have a short shelf life after harvesting, so you have to preserve them if you want to enjoy them for the rest of the year. I prefer to can plums to take care of both the flavor and texture. If you can with the pits, a little of the bitter substance is drawn out of the stone and puts a really good flavor in the plums. The most common plum varieties in Norway are Opal, Sugar Plums, and Victoria. Opal and Sugar Plums are ripe from the end of August until the middle of September, while Victoria Plums get ripe a little later, usually at the very end of September.

Cherries and Morellos

The sweetness and the acidity in cherries and morellos are an exciting starting point for many desserts and cakes. Cherries are divided into two groups: sweet cherries and sour cherries, and in Norway, we call sweet cherries morellos. Morellos are sweet and good and can be eaten exactly as they are. They can also be used in pies and desserts, for jamming and juicing, and for wine and liqueur. Cherries can be eaten as they are, and can also be preserved. Like morellos, they are also suitable for jamming, juicing, wine, and liqueur, and in this form they are also very good in pies and desserts. I like to combine cherries and morellos with almonds. The sweetness and bitterness in the almonds fits very well with the sweetness and acidity in cherries and morellos.

In Norway, we have a lot of good cherries and morellos. We export some of them also, because when the Norwegian berries are finally ripe, the morello harvest is long over farther south in Europe.

The small municipality of Lærdal in western Norway has become famous for its exceptionally good morellos, and berry experts from all over Europe come to study the growing conditions in this valley. The reason that Lærdal is so well-suited for morello growing, they explain, is that the nearby mountains hold on to heat, making it fit for precipitation, and that the days are long and light in the summer months. Therefore, Norwegian berries ripen very slowly and have a sweet and far more nuanced flavor than berries from more southern regions.

Rhubarb

Crisp, blushing rhubarb is a sure sign that summer has arrived. Rhubarb is actually a vegetable, but we use it in food preparation in the same way as fruit and berries. It contains too much acidity to be able to eat it untreated—even though many children probably still enjoy fresh rhubarb dipped in sugar—but it is ideally suited for juicing, jamming, and canning.

Carrot

The orange and resilient carrot naturally has a place in the sweet kitchen. Perhaps many think of the carrot as a dinner vegetable, but most people have tasted and liked a moist carrot cake. There is also no doubt that the carrot adds both sweetness and moistness to baked goods. Dry carrot cakes do not exist. Moreover, the carrot has a mild and round flavor that can be combined with most things. For example, I have a liking for carrot and orange, which is a combination that bristles with a bit of intensity. The color gets yellow-orange, the acidity in the orange is toned down, and the result is a milder and rounder orange flavor.

Apple Tart

You get the best apple cakes and apple tarts when you use Norwegian fall and winter apples. Apples with a lot of acidity and flavor are beautiful together with whipping cream with a lot of sweetness. I've chosen to make an egg stand here, which is a mixture of whipping cream, eggs, and powdered sugar. This forms the perfect counterbalance to the acidity in the apples at the same time as it ties the whole thing together.

Roll out the tart dough to a layer approximately ⅛ in (3 mm) thick. Grease the tart pan with cooking spray. Place the dough in the pan so that it covers both the bottom and sides. Then, put it in the refrigerator for 30 minutes.

Preheat the oven to 350 degrees F (180 degrees C).

Peel the apples, cut them in half, and remove the cores. Cut the apples into thin slices. Place the apple slices in the tart crust. Whip the powdered sugar, eggs, and whipping cream together and pour it over the apples.

Bake the tart for approximately 30 minutes, until the apples begin to take on color. Let the tart cool down in the pan at room temperature.

serves 4

1 tart pan with removable
    bottom, 7 in (18 cm) in
    diameter

1 basic tart crust recipe
    (see page 154)

2 apples
⅓ cup + 1 tablespoon (50 g)
    powdered sugar
1 egg (50 g)
⅓ cup (1 dl) whipping cream

Veiled Farm Girls with Cardamom

This is a simple and good dessert classic, and the result stands and falls with the quality of the raw materials. I prefer to use Norwegian apples because they have so much flavor, and they form a fantastic counterbalance to the fullness and the sweetness in the cream and bread crumbs. Cardamom is very good with apples and I think it adds the right something subtle, or that little extra, if you will.

Make caramelized bread, but bake it with a little ground cardamom. Let the bread cool and crumble it into crumbs.

serves 6
6 glasses with a capacity of 1
  cup (2 ½ dl)

caramelized bread
  (see page 156)

Apple Compote

Peel and core the apples. Cut them into pieces of approximately ½ x ½ in (1 x 1 cm) and place them in a little lemon water so they don't turn brown.

Put the apples, sugar, and ¾ cup (2 dl) water in a saucepan, and simmer over low heat, covered, until the apples get tender and begin to break apart. Flavor with lemon juice and cool.

3 apples, such as Gravenstein
¾ cup (150 g) sugar
¾ cup (2 dl) water
the juice from ¼ lemon

Cream

Lightly beat the whipping cream with the sugar and vanilla seeds.

¾ cup (2 dl) whipping cream
approximately 1 tablespoon
  (10 g) sugar
seeds from ½ vanilla bean

Assembly

First, place a little of the apple compote in the glasses. Then, add a little caramelized bread and whipped cream.

Nut Macaroons with Apple Cream

In Norway, you have many different types of nut pastries and macaroon varieties. Most of our macaroons are dry and can be kept for a long time. However, the macaroons I have made here are fresh. They can be kept a maximum of one week in the refrigerator, where they stay both soft and crisp. At regular room temperature they dry out and get just crisp. This macaroon is made with both hazelnuts and almonds, and it has a core of apple compote. I prefer using winter apples with a lot of flavor and tartness for this recipe, such as Gravenstein.

Run the almonds, hazelnuts, and powdered sugar into fine flour in a food processor and sift it. Whip the sugar and egg whites into a stiff meringue.

Fold the nut and powdered sugar mixture into the meringue with a spatula. Add a few drops of green food coloring. The batter must be mixed carefully so it doesn't collapse and get too loose.

Use a piping bag and pipe spots that are 1–1 ½ in (3 cm) in diameter onto a baking sheet lined with parchment paper. Sprinkle chopped hazelnuts over the macaroons for decoration.

Preheat the oven to 300 degrees F (150 degrees C).

Let the almond macaroons stand on the kitchen counter and dry for 20 minutes before baking them for 10–12 minutes.

Let the macaroons cool down before removing them from the parchment paper. They should be soft inside and crisp outside. If they get too crisp, they can stay in the refrigerator overnight.

makes approximately 40 pieces

¾ cup (100 g) blanched almonds
¼ cup (30 g) hazelnuts
1 ¼ cups (150 g) powdered sugar
⅓ cup (80 g) sugar
3 egg whites (100 g)
a few drops of green food coloring
approximately ⅓ cup (50 g) chopped hazelnuts for decoration

Apple Compote

Peel and core the apples. Cut the apples into pieces and boil them in water until tender. Drain the water.

Put ¼ cup (½ dl) water, lemon juice, and sugar in a saucepan. Add the apple pieces and the vanilla seeds and bring to a boil. Use a whisk and mash the apples. Mix the cornstarch with 4 tablespoons cold water and stir together. Add the cornstarch mixture to the apple compote and bring to a boil. Let the mixture cook for a few seconds until it thickens. Cool the apple compote in a bowl.

Put the macaroons together two by two with a little apple compote in between.

2 large apples
¼ cup (½ dl) water
the juice from ¼ lemon
¼ cup (50 g) sugar
seeds from 1 vanilla bean
1 ⅓ teaspoons cornstarch
4 tablespoons water

Caramelized Apple Cake

Caramel and apple is a classic flavor combination. I've made a twist on apple monks here, which are a type of bun with pieces of apple or apple compote. This delicacy became Norwegian about 100 years ago when it took a trip over the Kattegat Sea. To get the caramelized crust, you need metal pans with a capacity of approximately ⅛ cup (0.4 dl). Metal conducts heat well, and this is how you get the cakes caramelized on the outside and soft and moist inside. NOTE! The batter is thin and should stand overnight and rise.

Split the vanilla bean and scrape out the seeds. Mix the milk, vanilla bean, and seeds.

Lightly beat the egg and egg yolks together, and then whip it into the milk. Afterward, whip in the sugar. Stir the flour and cornstarch into the milk with a whisk.

Melt the butter and fold it into the mixture. Stir the rum in toward the end. Let the batter rise overnight. It can be kept for 2 days in the refrigerator.

Preheat the oven to 350 degrees F (180 degrees C). Grease the pans with butter.

Peel the apples and remove the cores. Cut them in ¼ in (½ cm) cubes. Put 1 tablespoon of the apple pieces in each pan. Fill the pans with the batter up to approximately ¼ in (½ cm) below the rim.

Bake the cakes for approximately 50 minutes. Take them out of the pans immediately after they are finished baking and let them cool on a rack. If they stay in the pans after they're taken out of the oven, they lose the crispy outside.

makes approximately
16 pieces

2 ¼ cups (5 ½ dl) milk
1 vanilla bean

1 cup (225 g) sugar
1 egg (50 g)
3 egg yolks (60 g)
⅔ cup (90 g) flour
3 tablespoons (50 g) cornstarch
approximately 1 tablespoon rum
2 tablespoons (30 g) salted butter
a little softened butter to grease the pans
1 apple

Apple Tart in a Dish

This is a sweet, crunchy, and delicious apple dessert spiced with cinnamon. It is incredibly easy to make, and probably also the dessert I make at home most often.

Mix all of the ingredients for the bread crumbs well in a bowl.

Soak the raisins in water for 20 minutes so that they take in water and get softer. Strain the water. Preheat the oven to 350 degrees F (180 degrees C).

Peel and core the apples. Cut them in slices and put them in a baking dish. Sprinkle on the raisins, sugar, and cinnamon. Wash the lemon and grate the yellow of the peel over the apples. Squeeze the lemon juice over the apples. Distribute the bread crumbs over the apples and put the dish in the oven.

Bake the apple tart until the top is golden, 20–30 minutes. Serve the tart hot or lukewarm, with whipped cream or vanilla sauce.

serves 4

Bread crumbs:
1 ¼ cups (100 g) whole, quick-cooking oats
¾ cup (100 g) flour
7 tablespoons (100 g) salted butter, softened
¾ cup (100 g) powdered sugar

2 tablespoons raisins
3 apples
3 tablespoons sugar
1 teaspoon cinnamon
½ lemon

Plum Compote

Plum compote is beautiful, and together with whipping cream it is a perfect dessert. Incredibly easy and very flavorful, pure and simple.

Cut the plums in half and remove the pits.

Put all of the ingredients in a saucepan and simmer over low heat until the plums become tender and begin to break apart.

Cool.

Serve the compote with whipping cream and sugar.

serves 6

10–12 plums, preferably Opal plums
½ cup (100 g) sugar
2 tablespoons (50 g) honey
⅓ cup (1 dl) water

Carrot and Orange Granité

Granité is the oldest form of ice we know. It is frozen fruit and berry juice that you scrape up with a fork and serve. Orange and carrot are two flavors that complement each other, and in addition, the granité gets a very nice yellow-orange color.

Wash and peel the carrot. Cut it into small pieces and boil it in water until tender. Drain off the water.

Bring the sugar and ¼ cup (½ dl) water to a boil. Pour the mixture into a bowl and chill it.

Put all of the ingredients in a blender and run until the carrot is completely blended. Keep the mixture in a bowl in the freezer.

When the granité is frozen (it takes 3–4 hours), scrape it up with a fork and serve it in a small, frozen glass.

serves 6

¼ medium-sized carrot, (30 g)
water for boiling the carrot
¼ cup (50 g) sugar
¼ cup (½ dl) water
1 ¼ cup (3 dl) freshly squeezed
    orange juice
1 tablespoon citrus liqueur,
    such as Grand Marnier

Plum Jam with Honey

Norwegian plums have a lot of acidity and flavor. The acidity is balanced nicely with honey. I like to use a robust heather honey.

Remove the pits from the plums and cut them into rough pieces. Put the plums, sugar, honey, and citric acid in a saucepan. Bring to a boil and let it simmer for 3–5 minutes until the plums are completely tender. Remove the pan from the burner and add Certo. Pour the jam into a freshly washed and boiled jar. Screw on the lid and set the jar upside down.

Cool.

makes 3 ⅓ lbs (1 ½ kg) jam

1 ¾ lbs (800 g) plums, such
    as Victoria
2 cups (400 g) sugar
⅔ cup (200 g) honey
½ teaspoon citric acid
1 bottle Certo (liquid pectin)
jam jar with screw lid

Pears in Lingonberry Syrup

Pears and lingonberries are two completely different flavors that I think fit really well together. Pears are sweet and mild, lingonberries are sour and sharp, and the result is exciting and balanced.

Peel the pears, then cut them in half and remove the cores. Place them in water so that they don't turn brown.

Boil the sugar and water in a saucepan and remove it from the burner.

Add the pears and the lingonberries to the saucepan and let it simmer until the pears are tender. Chill the pears in the syrup.

Serve the pears chilled, preferably with a spoonful of whipped cream.

4 pears, such as Gray pears
3 cups (600 g) sugar
2 ⅓ cups (6 dl) water
7 oz (200 g) lingonberries

Tip

Feel free to use apples instead of pears. Then, substitute the lingonberries with 1 cinnamon stick and 1 pinch of saffron.

Canned Plums

The Norwegian plum season is short, but we have massively good plums. If we want to enjoy plums the rest of the year, they have to be preserved. I learned to preserve from my grandmother. In the fall, she canned plums, pears, and apples with all the rules of the art. This recipe can be both doubled and quadrupled advantageously, but you still need only one vanilla bean.

Bring a large pot of water to a boil. When it boils, add the plums. Let them lie in the water for approximately 1 minute until the skins begin to crack.

Take the plums out and put them in cold water to quickly cool them down. The purpose of this boiling is so the skin will loosen and the pores in the plums will open so the sugar syrup can easily permeate the plums during the canning process.

Preheat the oven to 210 degrees F (100 degrees C). Use convection.

Split the vanilla bean and scrape out the seeds. Boil the vanilla bean, seeds, sugar, and water in a saucepan, and then remove it from the burner.

Pull the skin off the plums and place them in a boiled and sterilized canning jar. Fill it with warm vanilla syrup up to about ½ in (1 cm) from the top. Then, put on the rubber ring. If you use a jar with a clip lid, completely close the jar. If you use a screw-top jar, first tighten the metal band completely, and then unscrew the metal band about ¾ in (2 cm). This should be done so that the jar doesn't get too tight. It can, in fact, explode under heat.

Let the jar stand on a rack in the hot oven (convection) for 1 hour and 15 minutes. Take the jars out and set them upside down. If a screw-top jar was used, the metal band should be completely tightened before the jar is turned. The jar should be cooled at room temperature. Be careful not to let it stand on end or on cold surfaces like a marble table, as this might cause it to crack.

When the jar is cooled, you can take off the clip on a clip jar in order to see if the jar is tight. In other words, if there's a vacuum, you have canned correctly and the lid is secure. With a screw-top jar, you can screw off the steel band and see if the lid is securely on. If the plums are kept in a closed jar, they keep for 1 year.

16–20 Opal plums
1 vanilla bean
1 ½ cups (300 g) sugar
1 ¼ cups (3 dl) water
1 thin lemon peel
canning jar with screw lid or clip jar with a capacity of 1 pint (5 dl)

Rhubarb Jam

Wash the rhubarb and cut it into pieces of approximately ¾ in (2 cm). Put the rhubarb, water, and sugar in a saucepan.

Bring to a boil and let it cook for 5–7 minutes, until the rhubarb is soft and begins to break apart.

Remove the pan from the burner and add Certo. Pour the jam into a freshly washed and boiled jar. Put the lid on and turn the jar upside down. Cool.

makes 3 ¾ lbs (1.7 kg) jam

1 ⅓ lbs (600 g) rhubarb
¾ cup (2 dl) water
4 cups (800 g) sugar
1 bottle Certo (liquid pectin)
canning jar with screw lid

Rhubarb and Birch Sap Juice

Birch sap is not used much, but this tender, delicate juice is well suited as a cordial. Sap from birch trees is one of the first ones that can be harvested after winter. I usually freeze up the birch sap and mix it with rhubarb juice that I make a few weeks afterward. From the middle of April and throughout the month, you can tap birch sap, depending a little on where you are in the country. You cut off a branch the thickness of a little finger. It will begin to drip sap from the branch pretty quickly. Stick the branch down into a bottle and securely tie it to the branch with string. It takes about 1 day to get 2 cups of sap.

Wash the rhubarb and cut it into coarse pieces. Boil the water, sugar, and rhubarb, and let the mixture simmer for 10 minutes. Turn the heat to low and let the mixture simmer for 1 hour. Strain the juice. If it is used as is, mix 1 part juice to 1 part water.

Mix 1 part birch sap with 1 part rhubarb juice. It has a pretty short shelf life in the refrigerator, approximately 10 days.

The juice can be poured into plastic bottles and frozen.

Serve with ice cubes.

2 cups (5 dl) birch sap

Rhubarb juice:
1 lb 2 oz (500 g) rhubarb
    (approximately 6 stalks)
2 cups (5 dl) water
⅔ cup (125 g) sugar

Rhubarb Soup with Cinnamon and Sour Cream

Rhubarb is a sure sign of spring, and for me it is also a sign that the long-awaited Norwegian berry and fruit season is knocking at the door. When you make soup with the first rhubarb, you don't need to either strain the soup or peel the rhubarb. Cinnamon and rhubarb are very good, and a bit of rich sour cream on top makes the taste experience complete.

Wash the rhubarb and cut it into pieces of about ¾ in (2 cm).

Put the rhubarb, sugar, cinnamon stick, and water in a saucepan. Let it all come to a boil without stirring. Turn down the heat and let it simmer for 5–10 minutes until the rhubarb is soft, but before it turns into mush.

Dissolve the cornstarch in a cup with ¼ cup (½ dl) cold water and stir it into the rhubarb soup. Let it all simmer for 30 seconds until the soup thickens. Remove the cinnamon stick and put the soup aside to cool.

Beat the sour cream with the sugar and serve it together with the soup.

serves 8

1 lb 2 oz (500 g) red-stalked rhubarb
1 ¼ cups (250 g) sugar
3 cups (7 ½ dl) water
1 cinnamon stick
2 teaspoons (10 g) cornstarch
¼ cup (½ dl) cold water

⅓ cup (1 dl) sour cream (preferably Røros)
2 tablespoons sugar

Loaf Cake with Carrots and Nuts

This is a moist loaf cake chock full of good flavors, and it has crisp nuts that get it to crunch a little. Most loaf cakes you make by whipping butter and white sugar so that you get a light and crumbly cake. For my loaf cakes, I choose not to whip the butter, something that yields a firmer cake. In this variation I have also added grated carrot which makes the cake very moist. A little lemon and orange zest adds an acidity that works excellently with the mild, sweet carrot flavor.

Wash the lemon and the orange well in warm water before dividing them in half. Grate the peel of ½ lemon and ½ orange with the fine side of a grater. Avoid getting the pith.

Mix the sugar with the citrus peel. Mix the flour, nuts, baking powder, and salt with the sugar mixture in a mixer with a grind setting, or in a bowl with a wooden spoon. Add the whipping cream and eggs. Run it together until it's blended. Add the melted butter and stir the batter until smooth. Grate the carrot finely with a grater and stir it into the batter.

Preheat the oven to 335 degrees F (170 degrees C).

Fill a greased loaf pan with the batter and bake it for approximately 1 hour.

Take the cake out of the pan and let it cool.

Blend powdered sugar and lemon juice into a syrup.

Increase the oven heat to 475 degrees F (250 degrees C). Place the cake on a rack with a roasting pan underneath. Use a pastry brush and brush the entire cake with the lemon and powdered sugar syrup. Allow the cake to stand in the hot oven for approximately 1 minute.

1 loaf pan, 8 ½ x 4 ½ in (1 liter)

grated zest of ½ lemon
grated zest of ½ orange
1 ¼ cups (250 g) sugar
1 ¾ cups (240 g) flour
⅓ cup (50 g) coarsely chopped hazelnuts
1 teaspoon (5 g) baking powder
¼ teaspoon (2 g) salt
⅔ cup (1 ½ dl) whipping cream
4 eggs (200 g)
6 tablespoons (90 g) butter, melted
3 oz (100 g) carrots

syrup for glazing
⅓ cup (50 g) powdered sugar
the juice from ½ lemon

⋅Berries⋅

Just like with fruit, Norwegian berries are in a class of their own when it comes to flavor. And again, it is about light summer days, relatively low temperature, and a slow ripening process. In my bakery we are conscious of using the raw materials of the seasons, something which means that our products contain a lot of fresh berries in the late summer and early in the fall. When the season is at its peak, we still freeze a good share of berries, as well—to be able to use them the rest of the year. Berries that have been frozen liquefy and lose their shape, therefore I prefer to make purée out of them. Berry purée is nice to use in creams, cakes, ices, and jellies. Before the freezer was a common household feature, you had to jam and juice in order to take care of the fall berries. It's a good conservation method, and I also use them to find new flavor combinations that are good. Examples of these are blueberry jam with vanilla and raspberry jam with lychee.

❧ Blueberry

Norwegian blueberries have a lovely flavor that is so tender and mild that it quickly disappears in combination with other flavors. Juicing and jamming is the best method to safeguard the blueberry flavor, because then it doesn't need to compete with other flavors. I have experimented a bit in order to find flavors that don't overwhelm, but that lift and enhance the blueberry flavor, and vanilla is a flavor that just lifts and enhances, I think.

❧ Strawberry

Norwegian strawberries are the best in the world. Here, we find both garden strawberries and wild strawberries.

Among the garden strawberries, I love the Carmen, Corona, Frida, Gyda, Inga, Nora, and Oda varieties. In strawberries, sweetness and acidity are really well balanced, yet I think the truly sweet strawberries get better with a touch of lemon or orange. I prefer to use fresh strawberries in combination with crusts and creams. I think the berries are best-served like this, usually seasoned with anise and vanilla. When it comes to wild strawberries, they're smaller than garden strawberries and have a stronger, more concentrated aroma. I don't mix this rare flavor with anything; it must be enjoyed as it is.

❧ Raspberry

The raspberry is my favorite berry and is very versatile in the sweet kitchen. In addition to the freshness, it has a strong flavor of its own, and is sweet while at the same time containing a lot of acidity. These features make raspberries a fantastic raw material to work with. Among other things, I made raspberry chocolates with Norwegian raspberries when we won the Culinary Olympics in the fall of 2008.

The raspberry flavor is carrying, which is to say it doesn't disappear in combination with other flavorful ingredients, like chocolate or nougat, for example. Raspberries are also unbelievably well-suited in combination with cream products like vanilla cream, whipped cream, and mousses, among others. It is the acidity in the raspberry that provides a very good balance in relation to the fullness in these creams.

Raspberries grow both in the wild and in the garden. The wild raspberries are smaller than the garden raspberries and have a stronger and more concentrated flavor. These are the berries I have grown up with. Our family always went on berry walks in the fall. It was not necessarily as fun to pick the wild raspberries because there were a lot of thickets where they grew and it was easy to stick yourself, but this torment was without a doubt outweighed by the taste of freshly picked wild raspberries. The garden raspberries have better growing conditions, and get both sweeter and larger than the wild raspberries. They are also very good, albeit a little milder in flavor.

❧ Red Currant

The red currants that Rulle Rusk shook from Ibsen's bush are popular garden berries in Norway. Red currant is a hardy berry variety and it grows all over the country. As the poem of "Rulle Rusk" more than suggests, we have a long tradition of preserving red currants. Red currant is also ideally suited for jelly because it contains a lot of pectin. Otherwise, this berry is very good in cakes if you combine it with sweet and rich creams that round off the acidic red currant flavor.

❧ Black Currant

Black currants are a fantastic berry with their own strong and good flavor, and a great deep black-purple color. The black currant plant is similar to red currant, a robust, hardy plant, and it grows all over the country. Black currant is too sour to be consumed by itself, but it is well-suited for purée and juice. The black currant flavor is carrying, as with raspberry. That is to say, it does not disappear in combination with other stronger flavors like chocolate, for example. Therefore, I blend black currant purée with creams, and preferably in combination with chocolate.

❧ Lingonberry

The beautiful, red, and bursting lingonberries contain a lot of acid, and I use them modestly in desserts and cakes. Lingonberry has a robust and dominating sour flavor that I think is best suited as jam for dinner, next to the meat. It so happens that I also whip lingonberries with egg white and sugar into troll cream, which is a Norwegian dessert classic.

❧ Crowberry

Crowberries, or crakeberries as they're also called, have a robust and good flavor. The black, small berries are good when eaten naturally, and they have seeds too big to make good jam, but they are ideally suited for jelly, juice, and wine. My father made both juice and liqueur out of crowberry, and the result is brilliant. I usually blend crowberry juice, among other things, into my mulled Christmas wine. Crowberries grow in the wild in marsh areas, in pine and spruce forests, and in the mountains up to a mile above sea level.

❧ Cloudberry

The sight of golden, ripe cloudberries in a damp marsh is one of the most beautiful that exists. Cloudberries are an acidic berry with a very robust flavor. There are few flavors that can be combined with cloudberries, but sweet and rich whipped cream is beautiful with it. During the Culinary Olympics in 2008, we had great success with cloudberry chocolates made with milk chocolate and cloudberries.

Cloudberries are a berry you find only in the northern hemisphere. It grows wildly in marshes and moors and thrives especially well in our northernmost regions.

Since cloudberry only grows in the wild, it's a free-for-all for diligent berry pickers. It was a problem for a long time that cloudberries were picked before they were ripe, because there was such fierce competition for them. Therefore, in 1970 the Cloudberry Law arrived, which states that it is illegal to pick certain cloudberries.

In northern Norway there were many common places to divide the country into cloudberry patches. It was also forbidden by law to take cloudberries with you from another man's patch if the owner did not give permission. My wife's grandfather was a great cloudberry picker and had his own cloudberry patch on a small island in northern Norway. It was common there to have binoculars on hand so you could watch over the patch from a distance. Mercy to the one who wandered into another man's cloudberry patch!

❧ Sea Buckthorn

Sea buckthorns, also known as sea thorns, are acidic and fresh orange berries. They are too sour to be eaten by themselves, but they are well-suited for jelly, and sea buckthorn jelly fits together well with rich creams like vanilla mousse, for example.

Sea buckthorn grows on thorny bushes that can get up to sixteen feet high. In Norway, sea buckthorn is very widespread around the Trondheim fjord and as far north as Ibestad in Troms. It got the name "tindved" because we have used the branches for the teeth of a rake ("tin" being similar to "tann," the Norwegian word for "tooth"). The Swedish name "havtorn" (sea thorn) is significant because it thrives in the ocean sand.

Veiled Strawberry Girls

This dessert is obviously composed in the same way as veiled farm girls, only with strawberries instead of apples, and with cream and white chocolate. Strawberries and white chocolate are actually a perfect combination because the chocolate gives roundness and fullness to the strawberries, and the strawberries freshen up the sweet white chocolate. As with veiled farm girls, this dessert is very flavorful, and ridiculously simple to make.

Run half of the strawberries with lemon juice and sugar in a food processor.
Evenly distribute the sauce in the glasses. Cut the rest of the strawberries into rough pieces and evenly distribute them in the glasses.

serves 6

6 glasses that hold approximately 1 cup (2½ dl)

2 ¼ cups (500 g) fresh strawberries
the juice from ½ lemon
approximately ¼ cup (50 g) sugar

White Chocolate Cream

Finely chop the chocolate and melt it in a water bath or in the microwave (see page 137).
Cut the vanilla bean lengthwise and scrape out the seeds.

Heat ¼ cup (½ dl) whipping cream together with the vanilla seeds. Pour the cream over the chocolate and stir it with a spatula until smooth. Set the mixture aside to cool at room temperature.

Whip the rest of the whipping cream into a lightly whipped cream. Fold the cream into the cooled chocolate mixture. Carefully place the cream on the strawberries.
Add an optional layer of sweet rusk crumbs (see page 156) between the strawberries and the cream.

3 oz (100 g) white chocolate
¼ cup (½ dl) whipping cream
seeds from ½ vanilla bean
1 ¼ cups (3 dl) whipping cream

Marzipan Cake with Strawberries

There are countless varieties of marzipan cake in this country. In Trøndelag, the creation is "Lukket Valnøtt" (Enrobed Walnut), and in Bergen, "Hvite Damer" (White Ladies). When I make marzipan cake, I always blend plain whipped cream with vanilla cream. That way I get a rich cream with a lot of extra flavor. I prefer to fill the cake with fresh berries, and if it's the season, I use strawberries. This is how I get an exquisite cake with a good balance between acidity and sweetness. Last, but not least, I bake a soft and moist sponge cake which provides good texture. In my opinion, this cake beats both White Ladies and Enrobed Walnuts.

Cut out 2 sponge cakes with the cake ring, which should be 9 ½ in (24 cm) in diameter and 1 ¾ in (4½ cm) high. Put the cake ring on a flat dish and add 1 layer to the ring.

Fill vanilla cream up ⅓ of the ring. Halve the strawberries. Put them close together on the inside of the cake ring with the cut surface against the ring. The rest of the berries fill in the middle of the cake. Fill vanilla cream up ⅔ of the ring and add the last layer with the cake. Add a little vanilla cream and smooth off with a palette so that the cake is completely even. Remove the cake ring.

Roll the marzipan out thinly, and cut out a round with the cake ring. Place it on the top of the cake.

serves 14

1 basic sponge cake recipe
   (see page 154)

1 easy vanilla cream recipe
   (see page 152)

1 cup (200 g) strawberries
3 oz (100 g) marzipan

Strawberry Jam with Star Anise

Strawberry and anise are delicious together, and if you want to add an extra edge to the jam, you can add a tablespoon of Pernod.

Place the strawberries and sugar in a saucepan and mash lightly. Add the star anise and citric acid and bring to a boil.

Let it boil for 30 seconds. Take the saucepan off the burner and add Certo.

Pour the jam into a freshly washed and boiled jar. Replace the lid and turn the jar upside down.

Cool.

makes 3 ⅓ lbs (1½ kg) jam

3 ¼ cups (800 g) strawberries
3 cups (600 g) sugar
2 star anise
½ teaspoon citric acid
1 bottle of Certo (liquid
pectin)
jam jar with screw lid

Strawberry Tart with Oxalis Cream

You find many different varieties of strawberry pies and strawberry tarts, and most of them have a crisp crust, sweet strawberries, and rich cream. I have followed this model, but have made an extra-crisp and porous crust with an exciting, crumbly texture. I have also composed an entirely new cream with oxalis leaves. You can pick these leaves early in the summer, when they have an acidity that fits very well with the sweet strawberries.

Tart Crust

Melt the butter and cool to room temperature.

Beat the egg yolks and sugar until stiff. Stir the cooled butter into the egg mixture with a spatula.

Combine the flour and baking powder and fold it into the egg mixture. Place the dough in the refrigerator until it begins to firm. It takes about 1½ hours.

Preheat the oven to 320 degrees F (160 degrees C).

Roll the mound out to approximately a ½ in (1 cm) thick layer. Cut out circles approximately 8 in (20 cm) in diameter with a cake ring.

Place the tart crusts on a baking sheet with parchment paper, or in a tart pan 8 in (20 cm) in diameter.

Bake them for approximately 20 minutes until they are golden. Cool the tart crusts on a rack. I usually bake the layers in the rings I cut them out with. Then they are completely round.

Use a palette and spread the cooled oxalis cream on the tart crust.

Cut the strawberries in half and place them over the oxalis cream.

serves 6

1 cake ring or tart pan, 8 in (20 cm) in diameter

10 tablespoons (140 g) salted butter
4 egg yolks (80 g)
⅔ cup (140 g) sugar
1 ½ cups (200 g) flour
2 ½ teaspoons (12 g) baking powder

oxalis cream (see page 153)

1 cup (200 g) fresh strawberries

World's Best, My Way

World's Best, or Kvæfjord Cake, is considered a wholly Norwegian cake. It has a long tradition here in this country, but the actual structure of the cake can be found in classic cakes all over Europe. The combination of sweet, crisp meringue, a cake layer, toasted almonds, and vanilla cream is unbeatable. I am very fond of the traditional Kvæfjord Cake, but I think it lacks a little bit in the way of acidity and freshness. Here, I have made a version with strawberries and raspberries, which provides what I think the cake is missing and makes it even more unbeatable.

The recipe yields a cake of 9 ½ in (24 cm) in diameter. I use two layers for one cake. Each layer consists of a cake layer that you pipe almond meringue on before baking it.

serves 8

Cake Layer

Preheat the oven to 320 degrees F (160 degrees C).

Cream the butter and sugar until it is light and fluffy. Blend in the egg yolks and milk. Add the flour and baking powder and stir all of it until smooth.

Use a palette and spread out the batter in two 9 ½ in (24 cm) rounds, about ¼ in (½ cm) thick.

7 tablespoons (100 g) butter
½ cup (100 g) sugar
4 egg yolks (80 g)
¼ cup milk
¾ cup (100 g) flour
1 teaspoon baking powder

Make the Almond Meringue

Preheat the oven to 300 degrees F (150 degrees C).

Pulse the almonds and powdered sugar to fine flour in a food processor.

Beat half of the sugar and egg whites into a stiff meringue. Add the rest of the sugar and beat it in well. Add a few drops of red food coloring.

Fold the almond flour into the meringue with a spatula. Don't work it too much, because then the batter gets too loose.

⅓ cup (50 g) almonds
⅓ cup (50 g) powdered sugar
¾ cup (150 g) sugar
3 large egg whites (100 g)
a few drops of red food coloring
2 tablespoons sliced almonds

☞

Use a piping bag and pipe the mixture in the form of a spiral pattern on the round cake layers. Sprinkle the sliced almonds on the meringue.

Bake the layers for 15–20 minutes.

Allow the layers to cool off before you take them off the parchment paper. They should be soft inside and crisp outside.

1 easy vanilla cream recipe (see page 152)

Assembly

Place the first layer upside down. Spread the cream on the layer. Lay the berries over the cream. Put the other layer on the top.

½ cup (100 g) assorted berries, for example, strawberries, raspberries, red currants, blackberries, and blueberries

Raspberry Jam with Lychee

Lychee has a sweet and hearty flavor that provides the raspberries with a hint of flowers and makes the jam more exotic.

Run the lychee and syrup in a food processor.

Put the lychee, raspberries, sugar, and citric acid in a saucepan. Bring to a boil and let the mixture boil for 1 minute. Remove the saucepan from the burner and add Certo.

Pour the jam into the freshly washed and boiled jar. Replace the lid and turn the jar upside down.

Cool.

makes 4 lbs (1.8 kg) jam

2 ¼ cups (500 g) canned seedless lychees in syrup
1 ¾ cups (400 g) raspberries
4 cups (800 g) sugar
½ teaspoon citric acid
1 bottle Certo (liquid pectin)
jam jar with screw lid

Wild Raspberries in Vanilla Butter Cream on a Pistachio Crust

Wild raspberries are amazingly good. In relation to garden raspberries, they are stronger in flavor and have more acidity. The supply of these berries is sadly limited, but each year I make sure I get a few pounds. I like to combine wild raspberries with pistachios, because they are two strong flavors that supplement and complement each other. Pistachios were a luxury good for a long time here in Norway, which only got used in small, exclusive dessert cakes and pistachio marzipan. Today, everyone has access to pistachios and I use pistachio nuts not just in small dessert cakes, but also in large dessert cakes, like here.

The recipe yields 1 crust of 9 ½ in (24 cm) in diameter or 2 crusts of 6 ½ in (16 cm) in diameter.

serves 6

Pistachio Crust

Preheat the oven to 335 degrees F (170 degrees C).

Pulse the almonds, pistachio nuts, and powdered sugar into fine flour in a food processor.

Beat the egg whites and 3 tablespoons (30 g) sugar into stiff meringue. Add the rest of the sugar and beat it in well. Fold the pistachio mixture into the meringue with a spatula.

Line a baking sheet with parchment paper. Use a spoon and spread the batter out to a ½ in (1 cm) thick circle 9 ½ in (24 cm) in diameter.

Bake the crust in the middle of the oven for approximately 20 minutes. Try to lift up a little of the crust. If the parchment paper releases, the crust is done.

⅓ cup (50 g) almonds
⅓ cup (50 g) pistachio nuts
⅓ cup (50 g) powdered sugar
2 egg whites (60 g)
3 + 3 tablespoons (30 + 30 g) sugar

Use a spoon to spread the cream on the pistachio crust. Cover the cream with wild raspberries. Sprinkle coarsely chopped pistachio nuts and powdered sugar on the berries.

vanilla butter cream (see page 152)

1 cup (200 g) wild raspberries
2 tablespoons coarsely chopped pistachio nuts
powdered sugar for decoration

Raspberry Ice Cream

They began to produce ice cream in Norway in the 1930s, but in the beginning very few had access to this delicacy. After freezers became more widespread, the availability increased, and in the 1960s it evolved into a big industry. Since the freezer has become a common household feature, ice cream has become a part of people's dessert habits. It is first and foremost the ice cream factories that have been responsible for ice cream production here in Norway and not so many bakeries. In recent years, however, a steadily increasing number of bakeries have started their own ice cream production, and I think that's an exciting development. At my place, we distinguish between ice creams made with whipping cream and milk; sorbets made with fruit purée; parfaits, which are a type of ice cream that can be frozen without an ice cream maker; and finally, ices, which are made with fruit and berry juice, and also frozen without an ice cream maker. I prefer to make this raspberry ice cream out of wild raspberries, which have a heartier flavor of their own and are more acidic than garden raspberries. I add a little alcohol in order to lower the freezing point of the ice cream and thereby soften it a little.

Whip the sugar and egg yolks in a mixer until thick and light.

Make a water bath. Use a pot and a steel bowl that can hang inside the pot. The bowl must not be so small that it falls into the pot. Fill the pot with 1–1 ½ in (3 cm) water, put it on the burner, and heat the water until it simmers.

Pour the egg and sugar mixture into the steel bowl, and whip until the mixture begins to get warm and thicken. Transfer the egg mixture to the whipping bowl and whip until cooled.

Purée the raspberries in a food processor.

Add the purée and the vodka to the whipped egg mixture and stir it in well.

Whip the cream into a lightly whipped cream and fold it into the egg mixture.

Fill a loaf pan with the mixture and freeze it.

Take the ice cream out of the freezer and let it stand about 15 minutes in the refrigerator before serving. The flavor comes out better when the ice cream is not frozen solid, and it's easier to eat at the same time.

Serve the ice cream in a glass with whipped cream, or with Cream Cake with Red Currants and Raspberries (see page 73), fresh raspberries, sweet cookies (see page 85), or candied flowers (see page 133), optional.

serves 8

1 loaf pan, 8 x 4 in
  (1 liter)

5 egg yolks (100 g)
¾ cup (150 g) sugar
1 ¼ cups (3 dl) whipping
  cream
1 cup (200 g) raspberries
3 tablespoons vodka

Blueberry Jam with Vanilla

Blueberries have a very delicate flavor that can easily disappear when combined with other flavors. Vanilla, however, promotes and balances the blueberry flavor, and I have therefore made a jam with blueberries and vanilla, which I think is heavenly.

Split the vanilla bean and scrape out the seeds. Put the vanilla bean and seeds, blueberries, and sugar into a saucepan and mash lightly.

Bring to a boil and let it boil for 30 seconds. Take the saucepan off the burner and add the Certo.

Put the jam in a freshly washed and boiled jar. Replace the lid and turn the jar upside down.

Cool.

makes 4 lbs 3 oz (1.9 kg) jam

1 vanilla bean
2 lb 3 oz (1 kg) blueberries
4 cups (800 g) sugar
½ bottle Certo (liquid pectin)
jam jar with screw lid

Thick Lefses with Blueberry Butter

Thick lefses (tykklefser) are a variety of Norwegian griddle cake that are traditionally served with whipped butter and sugar. Here, I have replaced the whipped butter and sugar with blueberry butter. The idea comes from British lemon curd—you boil sugar, lemon, and egg together and round it off with butter. I have replaced lemon with blueberry, and this is, in my opinion, a perfect complement to lefses made with acidic sour cream.

Mix all the ingredients together and place the batter in the refrigerator for 1 hour.

Divide it into 8 portions. The batter is quite messy, but press or roll the lefses with flour to approximately ⅛ in (2–3 mm) thickness.

Fry the lefses in a skillet on medium heat, or preferably on a griddle, until they are light and golden on both sides.

serves 10

7 oz (200 g) Røros sour
  cream
⅔ cup (125 g) sugar
2 eggs (100 g)
1 teaspoon baker's ammonia
2 ¼ cups (300 g) flour

Blueberry Butter

Soak the gelatin in cold water for about 5 minutes.

Mash the blueberries or run them in a food processor. Put the mashed blueberries in a saucepan together with the sugar and eggs. Bring to a boil while constantly whisking the bottom of the saucepan so the mixture doesn't burn.

Squeeze the water out of the gelatin and stir it into the hot mixture. Stir the butter into the blueberry mixture and let it chill. When the mixture is cold, stir it with a whisk until smooth.

Divide the lefses into suitable servings and put them together with blueberry butter in between.

2 sheets of gelatin
1 cup (225 g) blueberries
1 cup (225 g) sugar
3 eggs (150 g)
9 tablespoons (130 g)
  unsalted butter, cubed

Spice-Preserved Cherries

Cherries with vanilla, anise, and cinnamon are very good flavors together that form the perfect complement to things like ice cream, chocolate, or whipped cream. NOTE! If you use frozen berries, do not thaw them, but pour the hot syrup directly over them in the deep-frozen state.

Split the vanilla bean and scrape out the seeds.

Put the sugar, water, star anise, cinnamon stick, and vanilla bean and seeds in a saucepan and bring to a boil.

Stir in the cornstarch thickener and allow the syrup to simmer for 2 minutes.

Pour the hot syrup over the cherries. When the syrup is cooled, add the strawberries and raspberries.

Let all of it chill at least 5 hours—preferably overnight. Remove the spices before serving.

1 vanilla bean

1 ¼ cups (250 g) sugar

1 cup (2½ dl) water

1 star anise

1 cinnamon stick

1 tablespoon cornstarch stirred into ¼ cup (½ dl) cold water

1 ½ cups (300 g) pitted cherries

½ cup (100 g) strawberries in pieces

½ cup (100 g) raspberries

Morello Cherry and Almond Cake

Morellos and almonds are flavors that complement each other perfectly. Almond cake has been made in Norway ever since we began to get access to the nuts early in the 1800s. Masarin cake is one of the classics and I'm using that as the starting point to make this moist, delicious fruit cake with vanilla cream and morellos. You can obviously use all kinds of fruit and berries, but if it's morello season, you definitely should take a chance. I prefer using morellos from Lærdal.

Put ¾ cup (2 dl) milk, whipping cream, sugar, and vanilla bean in a saucepan (the saucepan should not be more than half full); stir and heat to the boiling point.

Put the remaining milk and 1⅓ tablespoons (20 g) cornstarch in a bowl and lightly whisk it together. Whisk the egg yolks into the milk and cornstarch mixture.

Pour ⅔ of the hot liquid into the egg mixture gradually while stirring with a whisk.

Then, pour the mixture back into the saucepan. Let the mixture come to a boil and then simmer for 30 seconds while constantly stirring the bottom of the saucepan with a whisk so the cream doesn't burn.

Take out the vanilla bean after the cream has boiled.
Pour the cream into a bowl and refrigerate.

Preheat the oven to 350 degrees F (180 degrees C). Place the cold vanilla cream in a food processor together with the almonds, cornstarch, eggs, softened butter, and powdered sugar, and run it so that the almonds are finely chopped.

Put the batter, an approximately ½ in (1 cm) thick layer, in a roasting pan lined with greased parchment paper. Halve the morellos and remove the pits. Distribute the cherries over the cake.

Bake the cake until it's golden, approximately 25 minutes. Let the cake cool completely before it's removed from the pan. Serve with whipped cream, if desired.

serves 12

1 roasting pan, 12 x 12 in (30 x 30 cm), or 2 cake rings, 9 in (24 cm) in diameter

¾ + ¼ cup (2 dl + ½ dl) milk
⅓ cup (¾ dl) whipping cream
¼ cup (55 g) sugar
1 vanilla bean
1 tablespoons (20 g) cornstarch
2 small egg yolks (30 g)

1 ¾ cups (240 g) almonds
1 ½ tablespoons (25 g) cornstarch
3 eggs (150 g)
7 tablespoons (100 g) softened butter
¾ cup (100 g) powdered sugar

14 oz (400 g) morello cherries or cherries

Troll Cream with Jellied Cream

Troll cream is a gorgeous dessert made with stiffly whipped egg whites and lingonberries. It is generally served by itself, or in combination with cookies. Here, I have added a jellied cream to the troll cream, which brings a little fullness to it.

Jellied Cream

Soak the gelatin in cold water for 5 minutes. Put the whipping cream and sugar in a saucepan and heat it to the boiling point. Squeeze the water out of the gelatin, and melt it in the warm cream. Blend it together well and distribute the mixture among the glasses.
Put the glasses in the refrigerator to chill until the jellied cream firms.

serves 8

8 glasses with a capacity of approximately 1 cup (2½ dl)

¼ cup (50 g) sugar
1 ¾ cups (4 ½ dl) whipping cream
3 sheets of gelatin

Troll Cream

Mix all of the ingredients and whip until stiff and fluffy.

Gently fill the glasses with the firm jellied cream.

Serve the troll cream with sweet cookies, if desired (see page 85).

⅓ cup (1 dl) lingonberries
⅓ cup (1 dl) sugar
1 egg white

Variations

Troll cream can also be made with other berries. For example, try blueberry, black currant, red currant, or strawberry.

Caramel Pudding with Cloudberries

Caramel pudding is, for many, a primeval Norwegian dessert. When I, together with the National Culinary Team, won the Culinary Olympics in Erfurt in 2008, we made caramel pudding, among other things. It was indeed served in a slightly unconventional way, but had the same good and carrying flavors. When you take the culinary test, caramel pudding is one of the assignments you will most likely get. In order to get a passing grade, it is important that the caramel pudding sets correctly in the oven. It should not get too hot, because then it gets bubbles in it. Remember that when you get started.

Preheat the oven to 300 degrees F (150 degrees C).

Caramelize ⅓ cup + 1 tablespoon (80 g) sugar and put it in the loaf pan. Set a water bath in the oven. There should be enough water in the roasting pan so it stands as high as the egg mixture in the loaf pan.

Split the vanilla bean and scrape out the seeds. Put the vanilla bean, seeds, milk, and sugar in a saucepan and heat the mixture to the boiling point.

Whisk the eggs lightly together in a bowl.

Pour the heated milk into the eggs gradually while stirring with a whisk. Pour the hot mixture into the loaf pan. Put the pan in the water bath in the oven. The water should be so hot that it steams. Let the pan stand for approximately 30 minutes. If the mixture cools too much before it is put in the oven, it takes longer.

It is important that the mixture does not begin to rise, because then it is too hot. Nudge the pan a little to check if the mixture is firm. It should jiggle a little in the middle.

Remove the pan from the oven and let it cool for a minimum of 2 hours.

Sprinkle sugar on the cloudberries and let them stand for about 1 hour.

Serving

Invert the caramel pudding onto a platter. Cut slices of the pudding. Serve with sugared cloudberries and whipped cream with vanilla seeds. I also serve it with sweet cookies (see page 85).

serves 8

1 loaf pan, 9 x 5 in
  (1 ½–2 liters)

⅓ cup (80 g) sugar
2 cups (5 dl) milk
⅔ cup (125 g) sugar
4 eggs (200 g)

1 cup (200 g) cloudberries
½ cup (100 g) sugar

Black Currant and Semolina Cream

This is a dessert that came at the same time as the electric mixer. In fact, it must be whipped so intensely that it can't be done by hand. You make semolina pudding with black currant juice. When the semolina is finished cooking, it should be whipped until cooled. This makes it so the starch holds the air and the semolina is compact and creamy. I serve it with a little black currant jelly made out of black currant juice.

Black Currant Jelly

Soak the gelatin in cold water for 5 minutes.

Heat the juice to the boiling point.

Squeeze the water out of the gelatin and melt it in the heated juice. Pour the jelly in a bowl, and let it cool down and firm.

serves 6

6 glasses with a capacity of approximately 1 cup (2 ½ dl)

approximately ¾–1 cup (2 dl) black currant juice (blend ½ cup [1 dl] concentrated juice and ½ cup [1 dl] water)
2 sheets of gelatin

Black Currant and Semolina Cream

Boil the juice and sugar. Add the semolina and simmer for 10 minutes while frequently stirring the bottom of the saucepan so that it doesn't burn.

Put the mixture in an electric mixer with a whisk attachment and whip it until cooled.

Distribute the dessert among the glasses.

Serve with black currant jelly pieces and caramelized bread (see page 156).

2 cups (5 dl) black currant juice (blend 1 cup [2 ½ dl] concentrated juice and 1 cup [2 ½ dl] water)
½ cup (100 g) sugar
⅓ cup (40 g) semolina

Cream Cake with Red Currants and Raspberries

Sponge cake and whipped cream is a delicious combination, but boring. Therefore, you add an element; namely, berries. I think it's good to blend sour and sweet berries, like strawberries and red currants, for example. They are flavors that work very well together, in addition to forming a good counterbalance to the sweet sponge cake and the sweet, rich cream. Black currant also fits nicely into this flavor picture. I mash some of the berries, cut some in pieces, and let some remain whole. This helps the berries form an exciting texture in the cake. Most cover sponge cakes with cream, but here, I have decorated with a thin layer of meringue, which I have scorched light golden with a kitchen torch.

Assembly

Cut out 2 sponge cake layers with cake rings. Put the cake ring on a flat plate and put 1 layer in the ring.

Fill the vanilla cream ⅓ of the way up the ring. Put half of the berries on the cream.

Fill the vanilla cream to ⅔ of the way up the ring and place the last layer of cake on. Put a little vanilla cream on and smooth off with a palette so that the cake is completely even. Remove the cake ring.

serves 14

1 basic sponge cake recipe
(see page 154)

1 easy vanilla cream recipe
(see page 152)

1 ⅓ cups (300 g) berries
(I use red currants and raspberries)

1 cake ring, 9 in (24 cm) in diameter and 2 in (4 ½ cm) high

Meringue

Whip the egg whites and 2 tablespoons (20 g) sugar at half speed with an electric mixer or hand mixer until soft peaks form.

Add the remaining sugar and whip the meringue on high speed until stiff peaks form.

Spread the meringue over the entire cake.

Use a kitchen torch to give the meringue a golden brown color. Use the remaining berries to decorate the cake.

2 egg whites (60 g)
⅛ cup + ⅓ cup (20 g + 70 g) sugar

Juice Ice

When I make juice ice out of berries, I always freeze the berries first. The ice crystals break down the cell walls in berries and fruit and the juice runs out. It's an effective method to get the maximum juice out of the berries.

Juice Ice from Berries

Bring the water and sugar to a boil. Remove the pan from the burner and add the berries. Let the berry syrup soak for 20 minutes. Strain the berries and add the lemon juice. Pour the juice into molds and put in popsicle sticks. Using an ice cube tray is an option. Put the molds in the freezer until the juice is frozen.

serves 10

2 cups (5 dl) water
⅓ cup (80 g) sugar
1 ¼ cups (250 g) berries, such as blueberries, strawberries, raspberries, cloudberries, black currants, red currants
the juice from ½ lemon

Juice Ice from Fruit

Peel the fruit and remove the cores or pits. Cut the fruit into pieces. Bring the water, sugar, and fruit to a boil and let it simmer until the fruit is soft. Cool and flavor with lemon juice. Put the fruit mixture in a food processor and make a fine purée. Pour the juice into molds and put in popsicle sticks. Using an ice cube tray is an option. Put the molds in the freezer until the juice is frozen.

1 cup (200 g) fruit, such as apples, pears, plums, cherries
2 cups (5 dl) water
⅓ cup (60 g) sugar
the juice from ½ lemon

Crowberry Juice

When I was little, I always came along on berry walks in the fall and I thought it was terribly boring. Cloudberry picking was the worst because the cloudberries grew so scattered. Around the cloudberries were always plenty of crowberries: a huge patch of giant berries that would fill up my basket in a snap. One time, I gave in to the temptation to pick crowberries instead of cloudberries. I was quite pleased with myself when I had picked the basket full and could sit down and eat my packed lunch. My father was not so happy, because he didn't really know what he should use these berries for. He decided to try to make juice out of them, and it was a very good raw juice. So good, actually, that we've picked crowberries in our family ever since. I'm using the same recipe that my father invented at the end of the 1970s.

Run the berries in a food processor. Stir the berries, water, and citric acid together. Cover and place the mixture in the refrigerator for 2 days. Stir the mixture around approximately 2 times a day. Strain the mixture afterward through cheesecloth and measure it up. Add 2 ¼ cups (450 g) sugar per quart (liter) of juice.

Fill bottles with the juice and keep it refrigerated. The juice has a relatively short shelf life, about 10 days in the refrigerator. For a longer shelf life, it's best to fill plastic bottles with the juice and freeze it.

Mixing ratio: 1 part juice to 2 parts water. Serve with ice cubes.

2 quarts (2 liters) crowberries
2 cups (5 dl) cold water
1 teaspoon (5 g) citric acid
2 ¼ cups (450 g) sugar per quart (liter) of juice

Crowberry Juice
Pine Shoot Lemonade (see page 121)
Rhubarb and Birch Sap Juice (see page 32)

Sea Buckthorn Jelly with Cream

Sea buckthorn is an orange berry—or actually a fake fruit—that ripens in September. It was my berry-picking father who introduced me to sea buckthorn a few years back, and today I make several desserts with this bright orange, sour, yet good-tasting berry. Sea buckthorn is ideally suited for juice, which besides being healthy to the core, is very versatile as a starting point to make glossy orange cake glaze, creams, chocolates, and liqueurs. Here, I've made a jelly out of sea buckthorn and orange, which I serve together with a sweet cream to balance the sour flavor.

Run the sea buckthorn and orange juice in a food processor. Strain the sea buckthorn seeds.

Soak the gelatin in cold water. Put the juice and sugar in a saucepan and bring to a boil. Squeeze the water out of the gelatin and melt it in the heated juice.

Distribute the jelly among glasses and put them in the refrigerator until the jelly sets. You can optionally place the glasses in a container and tilt it so that the jelly sets on an angle in the glasses.

Whip the whipping cream with sugar and fill the glasses.

serves 6

6 glasses with a capacity of approximately 1 ¼ cup (3 dl) each

¼ cup (50 g) sea buckthorn, can substitute with ⅛ cup (¼ dl) orange juice
¾ cup (2 dl) orange juice
¼ cup (50 g) sugar
3 sheets of gelatin

¾ cup (2 dl) heavy whipping cream
1 tablespoon sugar

Drying Berries

Cookies and chocolates should be stored at room temperature, and they do not tolerate moisture. When I want to add fruit and berry flavor, I often use dried fruit and berries. What is left when the water is gone is concentrated flavor. You can use whole dried berries or fruit slices, mince them in small pieces and sprinkle them on, or simply crush them into a powder and sprinkle it on.

Lingonberries, black currants, and blueberries are dried as they are. Raspberries can be halved before they're dried.

I slice strawberries. Apples and pears I cut into thin slices and brush with a little lemon juice before drying. They can also be brushed with sugar syrup before drying.

Sugar Syrup

Bring sugar and water to a boil.

Cool.

⅓ cup (75 g) sugar
¼ cup (½ dl) water

Set the oven, preferably convection, to 140 degrees F (60 degrees C). Cover a baking sheet with parchment paper. Put a thin layer of oil or cooking spray on the parchment paper. Distribute the berries and the fruit slices over the parchment paper. They must not lie on top of or directly next to each other. Dry the berries and fruit in the oven with the door ajar for 4–6 hours.

✥From the Cow✥

All Norwegians know that Norwegian milk is the best of all. So, Norwegian dairies certainly produce world-class milk products, as well. When I traveled around the world and competed together with the Norwegian National Culinary Team, we always had Norwegian dairy products with us. You obviously find good dairies in other countries, as well, but even if the selection is much bigger as a rule, the quality of the goods is much more varied, like with whipping cream, for example. In Norway the reputation of dairy products is consistently high, and we have good, fresh products. It was with Norwegian whipping cream, Røros butter, and sour cream that I, together with the National Culinary Team, won both the Culinary World Cup in 2006 and the Culinary Olympics in 2008.

❧ Butter

Delicious, yellow, real butter is unbeatable when it comes to taste, and I use only pure butter in my recipes. Many choose to use margarine products instead of butter, but it gives a completely different taste and cannot be compared. I mostly use salted butter because salt is a flavor enhancer and I think that little bit of salty flavor promotes the other flavors in what I'm making. In recipes with a lot of butter, however, I choose unsalted butter and prefer to even add a little salt.

❧ Kviteseid Butter

Tine Dairy has begun to produce butter like it was done in the past, namely with cultured cream, or sour cream. The relationship between the amount of sour cream you use and how much butter you end up with is pretty lean. It is halved. Therefore, if you use "eight pots of sour cream," you get "four marks of butter," just like in the song about the old woman with the staff. There is higher water and salt content in this butter than regular butter and it is richer in flavor. In the past, butter was a regular form of payment and medium of exchange among people. You used to pay tax with butter, and the Tax Reform of 1617 was actually based on butter.

❧ Røros Butter

Røros butter is also made with sour cream and is characterized by its sharp flavor. You can make out the salt grains and if the butter is at room temperature for a few hours it will form water beads on the surface of the butter. If you want to be a little alternative and wish yourself a sunny summer, you can put out a little Røros butter on a winter day with sunshine. Our ancestors did it to thank the sun god and "butter" him up a little.

❧ Tjukkmelk (Dense Milk)

"Tjukkmelk" (thick milk), or "tettemelk" (dense milk), is a Norwegian phenomenon. Exactly how original dense milk was produced we don't know, but we suppose that one added common butterwort to the milk pail or in the sieve and then poured fresh, warm milk over. After that, the milk would stand for 2–3 days. That way it soured, but without separating itself into curds and whey. This was a great way to increase the shelf life of the milk. Today, we have no access to the original dense milk, but the Røros Dairy makes something similar that is called "tjukkmjølk."

❧ Whipping Cream

Whipping cream is absolutely indispensable in the sweet kitchen. It gets separated from the milk with the use of a centrifuge. Whipping cream is perfect in combination with sweetness and freshness. In that sense, strawberries with whipping cream are a perfectly composed dish. I use whipping cream mostly in the form of cream for cakes and desserts. Heavy cream is also perfectly suitable in the recipes in this book. When you beat cream into whipped cream, it's important not to beat the cream too much. If you continue to whip after it's become whipped cream, you beat the air out again and it will eventually separate.

❧ Sour Cream

The sharp sour cream flavor is gorgeous for many desserts. A good example is the classic Norwegian waffle with jam and sour cream. It is a perfectly composed dish.

Sour cream turns sour with the help of a bacterial culture, whether naturally or artificially added. Common types are light sour cream with 20% fat, and cottage sour cream with 35% fat. Because of the gorgeous flavor and the consistency, I prefer the organic Røros sour cream in my recipes.

Sweet Cookies

This is a sweet and tasty baked good that I make to give desserts and ice creams more texture. They're a little like goro (cardamom cookies), and you can bake them in a goro iron, a krumkake (Norwegian waffle cookie) iron, or on a baking sheet in the oven. They're not reserved for Christmas.

Preheat the oven to 350 degrees F (180 degrees C).

Mix all of the ingredients in a bowl, and stir it all into a smooth batter with a hand whisk.

Use a spatula or palette and spread out small cookies on a parchment-lined baking sheet.

Bake the cookies in the middle of the oven for about 3 minutes, or until they are light golden. Let the cookies cool on a baking sheet. They can be bent and shaped while they're warm.

A cake box is the perfect storage place for sweet cookies. They keep there for 2 weeks.

Another way to make the cookies is to put 1 tablespoon of batter in a krumkake iron. Bake until golden and shape them as desired. They can also be cut while they're warm.

⅓ cup (50 g) powdered sugar
⅓ cup (50 g) flour
2 egg whites (50 g)
3 tablespoons (50 g) unsalted butter, softened

Cream Puffs with Coffee Cream

Cream puffs are a crispy and luscious pastry that certainly created a sensation when they were first introduced. Because you boil the dough before you add eggs and bake it, it puffs up intensely. Therefore, it naturally gets a space in the center that can be filled with creams and berries, or whatever you might prefer. There are many classic pastries that use this dough as a starting point. Here I've chosen to make a coffee-flavored bread with coffee cream and almonds.

Bring water, salt, and butter to a boil in a saucepan. When it boils, take the pan off the burner. Let the pan stand with the lid on until the butter has melted. Set the pan back on the burner and bring the liquid to a boil.

Add the flour and stir with a wooden spoon until all of the flour is stirred into the liquid. Continue to stir until the dough gathers and pulls away from the sides. It takes about 30 seconds.

Remove the pan from the burner and let the dough cool for 2 minutes.

Stir in the eggs one at a time with a strong hand whisk or an electric mixer with a grind setting. It is important to mix well between each egg. When the dough is ready to use, it should be smooth and tough.

Preheat the oven to 350 degrees F (180 degrees C).

Fill a piping bag with the cream puff dough, using a star tip that has an opening of approximately ½ in (1 cm). Pipe the dough out into a shape approximately 9 in (22 cm) in diameter. Sprinkle the top with chopped almonds and pearl sugar.

Bake the cream puff for about 45 minutes, the first half of the baking time with a closed air valve and the last half with an open air valve. It is important that you do not open the oven door during the first half, because then the pastry will collapse.

If the pastry sounds hollow when you tap on it, it's done. Let the pastry cool on a rack.

Cut off the top of the cream puff.

Put coffee cream in a piping bag and pipe it into the pastry.

Put the top on. Sprinkle with powdered sugar.

serves 10

¾ cup (2 dl) water
6 tablespoons (90 g)
   unsalted butter
¼ teaspoon salt
1 cup (120 g) flour
3 eggs (150 g)
chopped almonds for
   decoration
pearl sugar for decoration

coffee butter cream
(see page 153)

Butter Cookies with Almonds and Røros Butter

These are one of the best cookies I know of. They contain a lot of butter and little flour, something that causes them to almost melt on the tongue. We have several varieties of these cookies—among others, butter cookies and butter wreaths. When you use a lot of butter, I think it should be a good butter that has a lot of flavor. Therefore, I've selected Røros butter, but dairy butter is also good. I also add almonds to these cookies, both because I think almonds are good, and also because they make part of the texture. Toast the almonds in an oven before using in order to get the maximum flavor.

Preheat the oven to 350 degrees F (180 degrees C).

Grind or finely chop the almonds and arrange them on a baking sheet. Bake until golden. Stir with a wooden spoon occasionally. Cool the almonds at room temperature.

Mix the butter and powdered sugar in an electric mixer or with a wooden spoon. Stir in the cooled almonds. Then stir in the egg and flour. Put the dough on a piece of parchment paper and put it in the refrigerator until firm.

Remove the dough and roll it to approximately a ½ in (1 cm) thick sheet. Poke the dough with a fork. Cut out rounds with a cookie cutter 2 in (5 cm) in diameter, or cut 1 ½ x 1 ½ in (4 x 4 cm) squares.

Put the cookies on a baking sheet lined with parchment paper and bake them until light golden, but still fairly light. It takes approximately 15 minutes.

Cool.

makes approximately
25 pieces

1 heaping cup (140 g) almonds
1 cup (120 g) powdered sugar
1 cup (250 g) Røros butter, softened
1 egg (50 g)
2 cups (260 g) flour

Puff Pastry Sticks with Brown Sugar and Cinnamon

Puff pastry is a classic baked good that has a long tradition in Norwegian baking. This pastry is an important part of the pastry chef examination, and there are probably more than a few who have wept over it. To get puff pastry to rise correctly is, namely, an art. It is folded, buttered, and rolled until you have 256 layers. Puff pastry in itself does not have much flavor, but it has a fantastic texture. You can combine it with savory just as much as with sweet, so this dough is used a lot in the savory kitchen, as well. It's filled with meat, fish, vegetables, and stews, and in the past there were many pastry chefs who worked supplying chefs with puff pastry. Now, industry has pretty much taken over. We make our own puff pastry in my bakery, but it is very tedious, so I recommend buying it from the freezer section. Here, I have made sticks out of it and flavored it with sugar and cinnamon. These sticks are good to munch on, and are ideally suited as an accompaniment to desserts with rich creams and sour fruit or berries.

Preheat the oven to 335 degrees F (170 degrees C).

Roll the puff pastry dough on a floured surface until it is ⅛ in (3 mm) thick.

Whisk the egg with a fork and brush it on the dough.

Mix the cinnamon and sugar and sprinkle it over the sheets of dough.

Use a pastry cutter or divide the dough into rods of ½ x 3 in (1 x 8 cm). Lay them on parchment paper and bake until they rise and turn golden, about 12–15 minutes.

Cool.

1 sheet puff pastry
1 egg
1 teaspoon cinnamon
¼ cup brown sugar

Variations

Replace the brown sugar and cinnamon with
· grated firm white goat cheese and paprika

· poppy seeds

· finely chopped nuts

· cinnamon and crushed, dried apples (see page 79)

Sweet Rusks

In Norway, there are many varieties of sweet rusks. They are a crunchy, crispy, and sweet little baked good that can be eaten alone or as an accompaniment to ice creams and desserts. In this sweet rusk recipe, I've chosen to use Kviteseid butter. It yields a slightly more sour and salty baked good.

Put the almonds and the hazelnuts on a baking sheet and bake them in the oven until they are golden. It takes about 15 minutes. Cool the nuts.

Mix the butter, sugar, flour, baking powder, and orange zest in an electric mixer. Add the eggs and mix together. Then, mix in the cooled nuts.

If the dough is soft, put it in the refrigerator a few minutes so it gets firmer.

Roll the dough into sausage shapes 1 in (3 cm) in diameter. Place the sausage shapes in the refrigerator for approximately 1 hour.

Preheat the oven to 350 degrees F (180 degrees C).

Put the sausage shapes on a baking sheet with parchment paper. There should be about 4 in (10 cm) between the sausage shapes as they rise and expand. Brush them with egg white.

Bake approximately 40 minutes until golden.

Take the sausage shapes out of the oven and immediately cut them in approximately ¼ in (½ cm) thick slices with a sharp bread knife. It is important to cut through, otherwise you just press the nuts through the slices. This has to be done while they're hot, otherwise it's no use.

Put the slices back on the parchment paper with the cut side down, and bake them for about 10 more minutes. Let them cool.

makes approximately
    30 pieces

¾ cup (100 g) blanched
    almonds
¾ cup (100 g) hazelnuts
⅔ cup (150 g) Kviteseid
    butter
1 cup (230 g) sugar
2 ¾ cups (380 g) flour
1 ½ teaspoons baking
    powder
grated zest from 1 orange
3 eggs (150 g)
1 egg white for brushing

Carrot Cake with Sea Buckthorn Cream

Carrot cake is a sweet and moist cake with a thin layer of cream cheese on top. This cake is very popular in Norway, and many bake it at home and make their own variations. I have also done that, and instead of putting cream cheese on the top, I have made layer upon layer of cake and cream cheese. This is how I get a light, fluffy carrot cake. I have also added some sea buckthorn purée to the cream which provides sourness and makes it a little fresher. If you don't have access to sea buckthorn, you can just as well substitute with oranges.

Cream Cheese

Soak the gelatin in cold water for a minimum of 5 minutes.

Put the sea buckthorn in a food processor and purée. Use a spoon and press the pulp through a sieve to separate out the seeds. Only the juice will be used in the cake.

Run the cream cheese, sugar, and sea buckthorn juice into a smooth paste in a food processor.

Heat the orange juice to the boiling point and remove it from the burner. Squeeze the water out of the soaked gelatin and let it melt in the warm orange juice.

Add the orange juice to the cheese paste and mix well. This can be done in a food processor.

Beat the cream into whipped cream and fold it into the cheese paste with a spatula.

Assembly

Use 1 round cake pan 6 ½ in (16 cm) in diameter and 2 in (5 cm) high. Grease the inside of the cake pan with a little neutral oil, such as soybean oil. This is so that the pan will release more easily.

Cut out two carrot cake layers with the cake ring. Put the round cake pan on a flat plate and put one carrot cake layer in the ring. Fill the cake pan up halfway with cream cheese. Put the other carrot cake layer on top. Fill

serves 8

1 basic carrot cake recipe
    (see page 155)

3 sheets of gelatin
½ cup (100 g) sea buck-
    thorn, can substitute with
    ¼ cup (½ dl) orange juice
9 oz (250 g) plain cream
    cheese
¾ cup (150 g) sugar
¼ cup (½ dl) orange juice
1 ¼ cup (3 dl) whipping
    cream

with cream cheese to the top of the ring, and smooth off with a palette so that the cake is completely even.

Let the cake stand in the freezer overnight or until it's frozen through. It takes approximately 6 hours.

Well packed, the cake can now be stored 14 days in the freezer.

Orange-Carrot Jelly

Wash and peel the carrot. Cut it into small pieces and boil it in water until tender. Drain.

Soak the gelatin sheets in cold water for a minimum of 5 minutes.

Peel the orange and run it in a food processor together with the carrot pieces into a fine purée. Put the purée in a saucepan together with the sugar and bring to a boil.

Squeeze the water out of the soaked gelatin and let it melt in the warm purée.

The jelly is ready to use. If the jelly is not used right away, keep it in the refrigerator. Then, warm it gently in a saucepan. Do not let it boil.

¼ medium-sized carrot, (30 g)
water for boiling the carrot
2 sheets of gelatin
1 orange
3 tablespoons (30 g) sugar

Before serving

Take the cake out of the freezer 4 ½ hours before it should be served. Cover the top of the frozen cake with orange-carrot jelly.

Let the cake stand for 10–15 minutes so that the jelly firms.

Warm the cake ring with a warm, moist dish towel so the ring loosens easily. The cake ring must be removed before the cake is set in the refrigerator to defrost. It takes approximately 4 hours.

Blueberry Sandwiches with Sour Cream

I picked up the idea for this dessert from our most beloved waffle. Waffles with blueberry jam and sour cream are fantastic, and here I have made an oven-baked waffle with almonds added. The almonds provide a crunchy crispness, and in addition to having a good flavor on their own, are just as delicious together with blueberries. I have mixed the blueberries into a sour cream–based mousse, and that's how I complete the flavor picture: waffles with blueberries and sour cream, in a new way.

Blueberry Mousse

Run the blueberries into a purée in a food processor.

Soak the gelatin sheets in cold water for a minimum of 5 minutes.

Split the vanilla bean and scrape out the seeds. Heat the vanilla bean, seeds, sugar, and milk to the boiling point.

Whisk the egg yolks lightly. Gradually pour the warm liquid into the egg mixture while stirring with a whisk.

Squeeze the water out of the gelatin sheets and put them in the warm sauce. Stir well so the gelatin blends with the vanilla sauce. Put the sauce aside to chill in the refrigerator or in a water bath with cold water and ice cubes.

It is important to stir the sauce at even intervals (every 10 minutes) until it cools to 70–75 degrees F (23–25 degrees C). This is to prevent the gelatin from clumping.

Whisk the blueberry purée and the sour cream together, and whisk the mixture into the vanilla sauce when the sauce has reached room temperature.

Beat the cream into whipped cream, and fold it into the mousse. Pour the mousse into a small loaf pan and put it in the refrigerator to chill until firm.

serves 8

1 loaf pan, 8 x 4 in (1 liter)

½ cup (125 g) blueberries
5 sheets of gelatin
1 vanilla bean
¾ cup (2 dl) milk
⅓ cup (90 g) sugar
2 egg yolks (40 g)
⅓ cup (1 dl) sour cream
¾ cup (2 dl) whipping cream

Oven-Baked Almond Waffles

Preheat the oven to 350 degrees F (180 degrees C).

Melt the butter and let it reach room temperature.

Grind or chop ⅔ cup (80 g) almonds to fine flour together with the powdered sugar in a food processor.

Add the egg whites to the almond and powdered sugar mixture.

Add the melted butter to the mixture, and then add the flour.

Cover a baking sheet with parchment paper. Spread the batter out on the parchment paper in an approximately ⅛ in (3 mm) thick layer. Sprinkle the almond slices and pumpkin seeds on.

Bake the almond waffle in the middle of the oven for approximately 8 minutes, until golden. Remove it and put it aside to cool. Divide the almond waffle into pieces.

Assembly

Put the pan with the mousse in warm water for a few seconds and invert the mousse onto a cutting board. Cut slices of the mousse and put them on plates. Put a piece of waffle on each side of the mousse slices like a sandwich.

8 tablespoons (120 g) unsalted butter
⅔ cup (80 g) almonds
1 cup (120 g) powdered sugar
3 egg whites (90 g)
½ cup (60 g) flour
2 tablespoons sliced almonds and pumpkin seeds for decoration

Dense Milk Pudding with Cloudberry Purée

If you want to make a perfect dessert for Easter vacation in the mountains, this is the thing. I was inspired by the mountains at Easter and ended up with dense milk from Røros and my father's mountain marsh cloudberries. I have also presented the dessert so it will be associated with eggs. In the old days, around Easter time, you celebrated when the hens began to lay eggs again. In fact, hens do not lay eggs in the dark season, and before one had the opportunity to lure them with artificial light, one had to make do without eggs for this period. So, the joy was considerable when it started to move toward lighter times and you could start getting eggs again.

Dense Milk Pudding

Split the vanilla bean and scrape out the seeds from half of the bean.

Soak the gelatin in cold water for 5 minutes.

Put the vanilla seeds, milk, whipping cream, and sugar in a saucepan and heat it to the boiling point.

Squeeze the water out of the gelatin, melt it in the warm milk cream, and stir well.

Set the milk cream to cool until lukewarm, then stir it into the dense milk.

Distribute the mixture among serving bowls.

serves 6

6 small serving bowls with a capacity of approximately 1 cup (2 ½ dl)

½ vanilla bean
2 ½ sheets of gelatin
¼ cup (½ dl) milk
¾ cup (2 dl) whipping cream
¼ cup (50 g) sugar
1 cup (2 ½ dl) dense milk

Cloudberry and Orange Purée

Run the cloudberries in a food processor. Strain the cloudberry seeds.

Pour the juice and sugar into a saucepan and bring to a boil. Add the dissolved cornstarch, and whisk it into the warm juice. Boil until it thickens. Cool and whisk in the cloudberry purée.

Put a spoonful of cloudberry purée on the dense milk pudding and serve with caramelized bread (see page 156).

1 cup (200 g) cloudberries
⅓ cup (1 dl) orange juice
⅓ cup (80 g) sugar
1 teaspoon cornstarch dissolved in 1 tablespoon cold water

Poor Knights with Dense Milk and Strawberries

Poor knights is a dessert you find in all bread-eating countries. In France it is called, characteristically enough, "pains perdus," or lost bread. The starting point for the dish is stale bread. When you dip this bread in egg, milk, or cream, put sugar on it, and bake it, the stale bread becomes a fantastic dessert. I serve poor knights with dense milk, a delicious soured milk from Røros. Some berries and sugar on the top completes the dish by adding freshness. This is how you save a loaf of bread from purgatory.

Dense Milk with Vanilla

Split the vanilla bean and scrape out the seeds.

Mix the dense milk with sugar and vanilla seeds.

serves 4

2 ⅓ cups (6 dl) dense milk
   (or something like Kefir)
1 vanilla bean
½ cup (100 g) sugar

Poor Knights

Cut the crust off the bread slices and cut them into pieces.

Whisk together egg, milk, sugar, and cornstarch in a bowl.

Melt butter in a frying pan.

Dip the bread pieces in the egg mixture and fry them in the butter until light golden.

2 bread slices
1 egg
⅓ cup (1 dl) milk
1 tablespoon sugar
1 teaspoon cornstarch
a little cinnamon
butter for frying

Wash and slice the strawberries. Sprinkle on a little sugar and toss it lightly together.

Serve the dense milk in deep bowls with strawberries, poor knights, and sugar.

1 cup (200 g) fresh
   strawberries
sugar

Barley Cream with Morello Cherries and Raspberries

Barley is a type of grain which is often grown in Norway. It is used mostly for beer brewing and animal feed, but has since old times been used a lot in soups and porridge. Barley has a good and exciting flavor, and here I have made barley cream, which can be reminiscent of rice pudding. Together with the morellos and raspberries, this is a simple and very good dessert.

Barley Cream

Put the barley in about ¾ cup (2 dl) cold water overnight. Drain. Split the vanilla bean and scrape out the seeds. Put the vanilla bean and seeds, barley, milk, and 1 tablespoon (10 g) sugar in a saucepan and boil on low heat until the barley is tender, approximately 45 minutes. Stir the porridge occasionally so that it doesn't burn.

Put the porridge in a bowl and cool.

Beat the whipping cream and 1 tablespoon (10 g) sugar, and fold it into the porridge.

serves 4

2 tablespoons (20 g) barley
½ vanilla bean
⅔ cup (1 ½ dl) milk
1 + 1 tablespoon (10 + 10 g) sugar
¾ cup (2 dl) whipping cream

Morello Cherry and Raspberry Salad

Split the vanilla bean and scrape out the seeds.

Halve the morellos and remove the pits. Place the berries in a bowl together with the vanilla seeds, sugar, and orange juice. Carefully fold all of it and let the salad stand for a minimum of 30 minutes.

Arrange the berry salad on a plate, and add a spoonful of barley cream next to it. Serve with sweet cookies, if desired (see page 85).

½ vanilla bean
½ cup (100 g) morellos
¾ cup (150 g) fresh raspberries
¼ cup (50 g) sugar
the juice from ½ orange

Alternative Serving

Distribute the berry salad in glasses and add the barley cream carefully on the top.

Nuts and Spices

Norway has many fantastic raw materials, but there is a lot we don't have, also. Throughout the ages many exciting raw materials have therefore—happily—come to Norway with merchants on the hunt for new customers. Many of these raw materials have become taken for granted here in Norway and are now considered Norwegian even though they aren't grown here. Among the recipes from my apprenticeship at the old and venerable Erichsen's Konditori in Trondheim are recipes that stem from the 1850s, and there are almonds, chocolate, and many kinds of spices in these. Creative bakers saw possibilities in the new food products and made, among other things, the first recipe for prince cake during this time period.

Common to all of the new raw materials was obviously that they had a long shelf life. They certainly had to tolerate long shipping without refrigeration. Nuts, dried fruit like figs, dates, and apricots, and spices met these conditions.

❧ Almonds

Almonds have fantastic flavor, and I use them in many of my recipes. In addition to the flavor, almonds provide an unbelievably good texture. There are both sweet and bitter almonds, but it is the sweet that are used the most and which are available in supermarkets. The sweet almonds don't contain amygdalin, which is a substance that converts to hydrocyanic acid when in contact with water. If you use bitter almonds, you have to let them lie in water overnight before use, so that the hydrocyanic acid is washed out. Bitter almonds are often used in small amounts together with sweet almonds in marzipan and chocolates in order to give the product a special flavor.

We also distinguish between Spanish and California almonds, even though California almonds stem from the Spanish. California almonds are used most today. They are pointed and a little hard. Spanish almonds have a rounder shape and are softer and better in flavor.

❧ Coconut

I mostly use coconut dried, in the form of shredded coconut. Besides providing excellent flavor, the coconut provides good texture. Shredded coconut tastes best if it is toasted in the oven at 390 degrees F (200 degrees C) for a few minutes until it turns light golden. Then it takes on a completely different flavor and aroma.

❧ Spices

In the sweet kitchen, the most commonly used spices are cinnamon, anise, ginger, and cardamom. Today, they are recognized and beloved flavors for most people, and in our time we also have access to these raw materials in the fresh form. It can be very good to combine the dried spices with the fresh. Gingerbread, which contains dried ginger, takes on a new dimension if you add a little fresh or preserved ginger.

❧ Dried Fruit and Berries

I cannot imagine a Norwegian bakery without raisins, dried figs, and apricots. The sweetness and flavor is well preserved by drying, but the freshness disappears. When I use dried fruit, like figs for example, I tend therefore to put it in water together with fresh raspberries. Then the figs get back some of their own freshness.

❧ Honey

Honey is the oldest sweetening agent that exists outside of fruit and berries. There are many types of honey, and we distinguish between two main types: flower honey and heather honey. The flower honey is light in color and mild in flavor and is in season quite early in the summer.

We have flower honey in Norway, but a lot of the flower honey is imported.

Heather honey comes later in the fall, and we have a lot of it in Norway. It is darker in color than flower honey and has a stronger flavor and aroma. I prefer the heather honey and think it's exciting to work with.

❧ Flowers

In the past, candying flowers was viewed as an important part of the pastry art, and you used the flowers as decoration for cakes. When you candy, you place flowers in sugar syrup, so that sugar crystals form on the outside of the flower. If you want to candy flowers, you have to be sure that the flowers you use are actually edible. In the Norwegian bakery, one first and foremost uses violets. There are few who keep the candied flower art alive today, but we have many edible flowers, and candying is a great way to preserve the fine, delicate petals.

Prince Cake

Prince cake is a delicious shortbread pastry that first saw the light of day in the 1860s at Erichsen's Konditori in Trondheim. This legendary bakery was established in 1856, and I was so lucky to get to have my apprenticeship there. The original prince cake recipe was a secret for many years. There were only a few at Erichsen's who got to use it. Now, as this bakery is closed and the possibility to buy the cake is gone, you shall get the original recipe from me. There are many good variations of prince cake, but this is moister than most others I have tasted, and it has a softer consistency that is reminiscent of marzipan.

Roll out the tart dough to approximately a ⅛ in (3 mm) thick sheet.

Grease the tart pan with cooking spray. Place the dough in the tart pan so that it covers both the bottom and sides. Then put it in the refrigerator for 30 minutes. The dough that is left over should be put in the refrigerator. It will be used to lattice the top of the cake.

Almond Filling

For brushing the cake, mix 1 egg yolk with 1 tablespoon water and set aside.

Preheat the oven to 335 degrees F (170 degrees C).

Run the almonds in a food processor until fine. Add the sugar and mix it in well.

Melt the butter and blend it in.

Mix the egg yolks, eggs, and whipping cream, and pulse until well blended.

Fill the tart pan with the almond mixture.

Roll out the remaining dough and cut it in thin strips with a pastry cutter.

Place the strips in a lattice pattern on the top of the cake. Brush the top of the cake with the egg yolk mixture.

Bake the cake until golden, approximately 40 minutes.

Allow the cake to cool in the pan at room temperature.

serves 6

1 tart pan with removable base, 8 in (20 cm) in diameter

1 basic tart crust recipe (see page 154)

1 ¾ cups (220 g) almonds
1 cup (200 g) sugar
1 tablespoon (20 g) butter
1 egg yolk (20 g)
1 egg (50 g)
¼ cup (½ dl) whipping cream

For brushing the cake
1 egg yolk mixed with 1 tablespoon water

Wreath Cake Tart with Strawberries and Anise Cream

We eat wreath cake for Christmas and on May 17 (Norwegian Constitution Day), and we often serve it with strawberries and coffee, or with a glass of good dessert wine. Here, I have made a wreath cake the crust for vanilla cream and sweet, fresh strawberries. I have also added a little anise, which I think is lovely with strawberries. If you want to go a step further, you can add a tablespoon of Pernod in the cream. You can serve this cake with anything at all.

Wreath Cake Dough

Run the almonds, sugar, and powdered sugar in a food processor so that they get completely minced. Knead in the egg white until the dough is smooth. It should be firm. Remove ¾ cup (150 g) for the wreath cake tart filling. Roll the dough that's left into a sausage shape, approximately 1 in (2 cm) thick, and shape it into a circle that is 7 in (18 cm) in diameter. Place it on a baking sheet with parchment paper.

serves 6

1 ¼ cups (160 g) blanched almonds
1 ¼ cups (150 g) powdered sugar
⅓ cup (60 g) sugar
1 egg white (30 g)

Wreath Cake Tart Filling

Preheat oven to 350 degrees F (180 degrees C).

Mix the wreath cake dough and egg in a food processor until it forms a smooth batter.

Fill the wreath cake ring with the mixture and bake it until golden, about 20 minutes.

Let the cake cool at room temperature.

Make anise cream (see page 152) and refrigerate.

Spread the cold anise cream on the wreath cake tart. Cover with sliced strawberries.

¾ cup (150 g) wreath cake dough
1 egg

anise cream (see page 152)

1 cup (200 g) fresh strawberries

Coconut Balls

Coconut balls are perfectly composed when it comes to texture, but I think they're lacking in flavor a little. When I make coconut balls, I bake the cookies myself. I toast the coconut to bring out more flavor, and I add honey to the meringue. Meringue is so sweet that it's important to use a dark chocolate with it. I prefer to use one with 60–70% cocoa solids, which can really form a counterbalance to the sweetness. The result of this adjustment is, in my opinion, a completely perfect coconut ball.

Cookies

Preheat the oven to 350 degrees F (180 degrees C).

Mix all of the ingredients in a bowl, and stir it all into a smooth batter with a hand whisk.

Use a spatula or palette and spread out small cookies on a baking sheet lined with parchment paper.

Bake the cookies in the middle of the oven for approximately 3 minutes, or until they are light golden. Let the cookies cool on the baking sheet.

A cake box is the perfect storage place for the cookies. They keep there for 2 weeks.

makes approximately
20 pieces

⅓ cup (50 g) powdered
sugar
⅓ cup (50 g) flour
2 egg whites (50 g)
3 tablespoons (50 g)
unsalted butter, softened

Coconut Meringue

Preheat the oven to 320 degrees F (160 degrees C).

Put the shredded coconut on a baking sheet and toast it in the oven until golden, approximately 10 minutes.

Whisk the egg white and honey to soft peaks at half speed with an electric mixer or with a hand mixer.

Place the sheets of gelatin in a bowl with cold water.

⅓ cup, packed (50 g)
shredded coconut
2 egg whites (50 g)
1 tablespoon (20 g) heather
honey
1 sheet of gelatin
½ cup (100 g) sugar
¼ cup (½ dl) water

Mix the sugar with ¼ cup (½ dl) water in a saucepan and let it come to a rolling boil for 4–5 minutes without stirring until it turns into syrup. When it forms foam along the edge of the saucepan, remove it with a spoon. If you have a candy thermometer, it should read 248 degrees F (120 degrees C). If not, you can do the ball test: put a little syrup on a teaspoon and dip it in a cup of cold water. After a few seconds you should be able to roll a soft ball of syrup, if the temperature is right. If the syrup is too soft to roll a ball with, it has to boil longer. If it's too hard, so that you can't roll a ball, the temperature is too high. Then, you can try adding a little water and stir it into the syrup. This can, however, lead to the sugar crystallizing, and then it just has to be discarded.

Pour the boiled syrup in a thin stream into the half-whisked egg whites while the mixer runs at half speed. It is important that the sugar syrup falls right down into the meringue and not onto the whisk. If the sugar syrup hits the whisk, throw the sugar syrup out to the side of the bowl.

Then, whip the meringue on full speed for about 30 seconds until it gets fluffy. It should still be warm.

Squeeze the water out of the sheet of gelatin and whip it well into the warm meringue.

Stir in the coconut with a spatula.
Put the coconut meringue into a piping bag and pipe it onto the cookies. You can also sprinkle them with coconut or dip them in tempered dark chocolate (see page 137).

Small Coconut Balls

Make coconut meringue. Add a few drops of yellow food coloring, optional, and stir well. Sprinkle the parchment paper with powdered sugar. Put the coconut meringue on the parchment paper and sprinkle it with powdered sugar. Use your hands to press the meringue flat. Let it stand until it firms. Cut the meringue into cubes of approximately ¾ x ¾ in (2 x 2 cm) and roll them in powdered sugar. Shake off excess powdered sugar.

Coconut Macaroons with Egg Nog

When I went into training as a pastry chef at Erichsen Konditori in Trondheim, I made tons of coconut macaroons when it got close to Christmas. In the bakery, coconut macaroons were served with egg nog and coffee on a large scale. I have experimented a bit with these macaroons and have come up with a variation that is softer and airier than what I made for the pastry chef examination. In addition, I have made a cream with egg nog to put inside. It turns these macaroons into the ultimate Christmas cake for me.

Run the almonds, coconut, and powdered sugar into fine flour in a food processor and sift it.

Whip the sugar and egg whites into a stiff meringue.

Fold the almond mixture into the meringue with a spatula.

Use a piping bag and pipe spots that are 1 ½ in (4 cm) in diameter onto a baking sheet lined with parchment paper. Sprinkle the coconut over the macaroons as decoration.

Preheat the oven to 335 degrees F (170 degrees C).

Let the almond macaroons stand on the kitchen counter and dry for 20 minutes before you bake them for 15–20 minutes.

Let the macaroons cool completely before you take them off the parchment paper. They should be soft inside and crisp outside. If they get too crisp they can be put in the refrigerator overnight.

makes approximately 40 pieces

¾ cup (100 g) blanched almonds
¼ cup (30 g) shredded coconut
1 ¼ cups (150 g) powdered sugar
⅓ cup (80 g) sugar
3 egg whites (100 g)
approximately ⅓ cup, packed (50 g) shredded coconut for decoration

Egg Nog Cream

Whip the egg yolks and 1 tablespoon (10 g) sugar until frothy. Add the softened butter and whisk the mixture until thick and light. Whip the egg whites and 3 tablespoons (30 g) sugar into a meringue. Fold the meringue into the butter mixture with a spatula and flavor with the egg nog.

Put the macaroons together two by two with a little egg nog cream in between.

2 egg yolks (40 g)
1 tablespoon (10 g) sugar
3 tablespoons (50 g) unsalted butter, softened
2 egg whites (60 g)
3 tablespoons (30 g) sugar
2 tablespoons (20 g) egg nog

Egg Nog

I usually make egg nog for Christmas. I quite simply make a vanilla sauce that I add liquor to, such as blending chilled vanilla sauce with vodka. I prefer to store the nog in bottles in the refrigerator. The nog thickens when it stands, so it's important to shake it well before use.

Vanilla Sauce

This is a basic sauce that is the starting point for many sauces and desserts and the base for egg nog. It is important to be careful when a sauce is thickened or warmed so that it doesn't separate. Take the saucepan off the burner several times during the warming so that you have control of the temperature. Be sure to have a bowl and sieve on hand before you begin to thicken the sauce.

Split the vanilla bean and scrape out the seeds.

Heat the milk, whipping cream, vanilla bean, seeds, and half of the sugar to the boiling point.

Lightly whisk the egg yolks and the remaining sugar together.

Pour the hot liquid into the egg mixture gradually while stirring with a whisk. Then, pour the sauce back into the saucepan.

Heat the sauce while stirring the bottom of the saucepan with a spatula. It is important to stir the entire time to prevent the egg yolks from hardening in the bottom of the pan.

When the sauce thickens, 183–185 degrees F (84–85 degrees C) on a thermometer, strain it into a bowl. To see if the sauce is thick enough, lift sauce up on a spatula and drag a finger through it. If the sauce doesn't flow together again, it's ready.

Chill the sauce in the refrigerator.

makes 1 quart (1 liter)

1 cup (2 ½ dl) 60%
   (120 proof) vodka
1 vanilla bean
1 cup (2 ½ dl) milk
1 cup (2 ½ dl) whipping
   cream
1 cup (200 g) sugar
5 egg yolks (100 g)

Tip

When you warm milk and whipping cream for something like vanilla sauce, it is important that it does not boil, but is only heated to the boiling point. Boiled milk doesn't taste particularly good.

Pine Shoot Lemonade

If you want a slightly different lemonade, this could be the thing. Pine shoots (the small offshoots of new growth at the end of pine branches) have a sour flavor, but you have to pick them early, otherwise they get too much tree flavor in the drink.

Pick pine shoots early in the spring while they're light green and completely soft. They should not be longer than about ¾ in (2 cm).

Bring the sugar and water to a boil. Put in the pine shoots and let them infuse for 15 minutes. Drain the syrup and put it in the refrigerator.

makes ½ gallon (2 liters)

⅓ cup (1 dl) pine shoots
¼ cup (50 g) sugar
2 cups (5 dl) water

Bring the sugar and water to a boil and cool down.

Wash the lemons well and cut them into rough pieces. Juice the lemon and put both peel and juice in the sugar syrup. Let the syrup stand overnight in the refrigerator. Strain the lemon rinds.

Blend the pine shoot syrup and the lemonade.

This lemonade has a pretty short shelf life in the refrigerator, about 10 days, but can be poured into plastic bottles and frozen.

2 cups (400 g) sugar
1 ⅔ cups (4 dl) water
2 large lemons

Serving

Mix 1 part lemonade with 2 parts water. Serve with ice cubes.

Success Tart with Lemon

Success tart is a delicious coffee cake that many bake at home. Therefore, there are quite a few local varieties. For example, it is served both with and without chocolate. My success tart has dark chocolate glaze. I have also added some lemon to the cream to freshen it up a little.

Make the basic almond cake (see page 155).

Lemon Cream

Whisk together all of the ingredients except for the butter in a saucepan. Heat the mixture to the boiling point while constantly whisking.

Let the mixture simmer for about 20 seconds until it gets thick and smooth. Stir the bottom of the saucepan constantly with a whisk so that the cream doesn't burn.

Pour the mixture into a bowl. Stir the butter into the warm lemon cream with a hand whisk. It is important to mix in the butter while it melts.

Cool.

Pour the mixture into a bowl. Cover with plastic and put the cream in the refrigerator to chill.

Assembly

1 cake ring, 6 ½ in (16 cm) in diameter

Cut out three almond cake layers with the cake ring. Put the round cake pan on a flat plate and put a layer of almond cake in the pan.

Fill the pan up ⅓ with lemon cream. Add another layer of almond cake. Fill the pan up ⅔ with lemon cream and add the last layer of almond cake. Add a little lemon cream, and spread it with a palette so that the cake is completely smooth. Remove the cake ring.

Serving

The cake can be decorated with grated chocolate or chocolate glaze (see page 157).

serves 6 people

1 basic almond cake recipe
  (see page 155)

¼ cup (½ dl) milk
⅓ cup (¾ dl) freshly
  squeezed lemon juice
½ cup (100 g) sugar
1 large egg (70 g)
4 egg yolks (80 g)
2 teaspoons (10 g) corn-
  starch
5 tablespoons (80 g) cold
  unsalted butter, cubed

Orange Marmalade with Cinnamon

Peel the oranges and roughly chop the fruit in a food processor.

Place it in a saucepan together with the sugar and grapefruit juice and let it come to a boil. Remove the foam with a ladle.

Split the vanilla bean and scrape out the seeds. Add the cinnamon stick, vanilla bean and seeds, and the fruit mixture, and bring it to a boil. Remove the saucepan and add Certo.

Let the marmalade stand on the kitchen counter for 30 minutes. Stir it 2–3 times so that the pulp doesn't lie on the top.

Fill a clean jam jar with the marmalade.

makes 4 lbs 3 oz (1.9 kg)
  marmalade

1 ⅓ lbs (600 g) oranges
6 cups (1.2 kg) sugar
¾ cup (2 dl) freshly
  squeezed red grapefruit
  juice
1 vanilla bean
1 cinnamon stick
1 bottle Certo (liquid pectin)

Fig Jam with Raspberries

Dried figs are sweet and good, and like most other Norwegians, I eat them for Christmas. This fig jam is made of only dried figs, and I compensate for the missing freshness with a little raspberry.

Cut the stems off the dried figs and cut them into rough pieces. Then pour on the water and set the figs in the refrigerator overnight. Place the figs with water in a food processor and run it into a purée.

Mix the figs, sugar, and raspberries in a saucepan and bring to a boil. Let it boil for 30 seconds. Take the saucepan off the burner and add Certo. Place the jam in a freshly washed and boiled jar. Put on the lid and turn the jar upside down.

Cool.

makes 2 lbs 3 oz (1 kg) jam

9 oz (250 g) dried figs
1 cup (2 ½ dl) water
1 ½ cups (300 g) sugar
½ cup (100 g) raspberries
½ bottle Certo (liquid pectin)
jam jar with screw lid

Marzipan Fruit

You can make marzipan yourself, or you can buy it already made. If you buy it, you have to look at the almond content. I think marzipan should contain 40–50% almonds. The rest is mostly sugar. I don't like that the almond flavor gets overshadowed by sugar. In many marzipans the almonds are also substituted with apricot kernels. Making marzipan was one of the permanent Christmas preparations at home when I was little. Christmas was approaching when my father began to blanch the almonds and place them to dry in the kitchen cabinet. I always got to help with making marzipan fruit and figures. We also used to dip marzipan balls in chocolate. Now, I add flavor to marzipan with grated orange peel, liqueurs, and chopped nuts.

Marzipan

Run the almonds and powdered sugar in a food processor so that they get completely ground. Knead the egg white in until the mixture gets smooth. Mix the marzipan well with Grand Marnier.

Roll the marzipan into balls by tablespoons. After you have rolled the balls, you can shape different fruits. Brush them with food coloring and set them to dry.

makes approximately 20 pieces

1 ¼ cups (160 g) blanched almonds
1 ⅔ cups (200 g) powdered sugar
1 egg white (30 g)
¼ cup Grand Marnier liqueur
food coloring

Coloring of Marzipan

Many color the marzipan before they make the figures, but I have found out that it is better to shape the marzipan first and then apply color. I quite simply use a brush and paint the figures. That way I get stronger color at the same time as I use less food coloring.

It may be wise to let the marzipan dry a few hours before you begin to paint it. Then, the color absorbs more quickly and it doesn't run. You can also roll the fully formed marzipan in powdered sugar, like I've done with the apricots in the picture. To do this, I place the newly colored and wet figures in powdered sugar and turn them around. After that, I shake off the excess. That way I get a nice matte finish that is a little like apricot skin.

Crystallized Marzipan

Put the sugar and water in a saucepan. Boil until the sugar is dissolved, and set the syrup aside to cool.

2 ½ cups (500 g) sugar
1 cup (2 ½) dl water

Place the marzipan fruit upside down in the cooled sugar syrup. Let stand for a minimum of 24 hours.
Lift them out and place on paper towels to drain. The marzipan is now crystallized sugar.

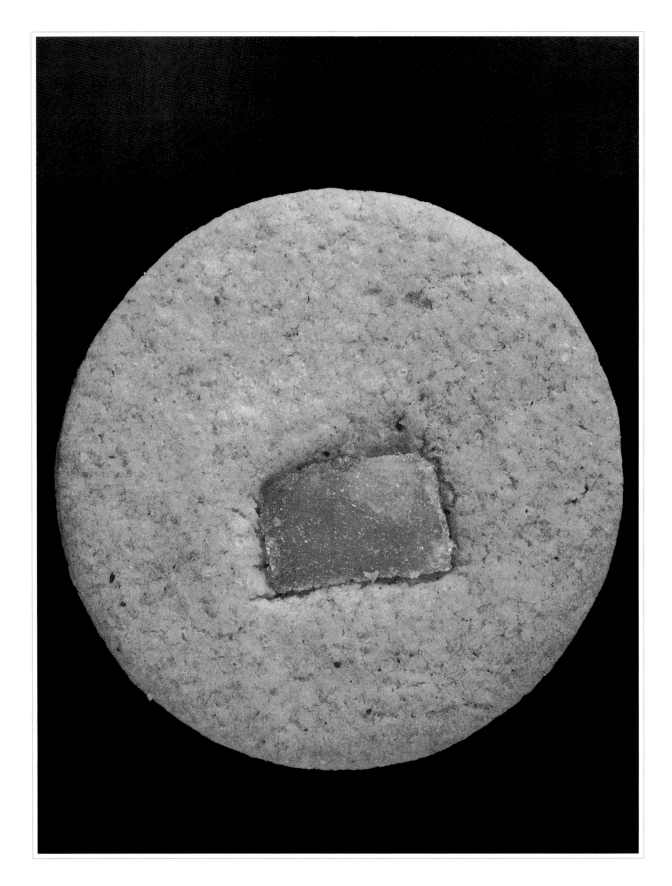

Ginger Cookies

These are an offspring of ginger snaps or molasses snaps, which are cookies made with molasses and butter. In Norway, it has long been a tradition to use dried ginger in baked goods. It has a good, sharp flavor, which I have highlighted here with the help of cinnamon and pepper. In addition, I have added a piece of candied ginger, which adds other flavor nuances of ginger.

Put molasses and sugar in a saucepan, and heat it until it becomes fluid.

Remove the saucepan from the burner and add the butter. Stir until the butter is melted.

Mix the spices with flour, and stir it into the molasses mixture with a wooden spoon, or in an electric mixer with an attachment.

Put the mixture on a sheet of parchment paper and put it in the refrigerator until it gets firm.

Preheat the oven to 335 degrees F (170 degrees C).

Remove the mixture and roll it until it is about ¼ in (½ cm) thick. Cut out circles with a cookie cutter 2 in (5 cm) in diameter, or cut squares of 1 ½ x 1 ½ in (4 x 4 cm). Place the cookies on a baking sheet with parchment paper. Optionally, cut small pieces of candied ginger, and place some of the pieces on each of the cookies. Bake them for 15–20 minutes.

Cool.

makes approximately
  40 pieces

¾ cup (150 g) dark molasses
¾ cup (150 g) brown sugar
⅔ cup (150 g) butter
3 ⅓ cups (450 g) flour
2 teaspoons ground
  cinnamon
1 teaspoon ground ginger
2 eggs (100 g)
candied ginger, optional

Marshmallows with Heather Honey

Marshmallows are foam-like and good to chew on. The texture makes them a good accompaniment to desserts with a crisp crust, soft creams, and tart jellies. The taste, however, is pretty boring. I have therefore experimented a good deal to put flavor in these foamy pads. Heather honey is well-suited because it provides sweetness in addition to good flavor. Marshmallows with heather honey are included in the selection of goods in my shop. I also make variations where I add chopped nuts, vanilla seeds, berry syrups, and toasted coconut. The result is marshmallows that have both good texture and exciting flavor.

Soak the gelatin in cold water for 10 minutes.

Whisk the egg whites and honey to soft peaks on half speed in an electric mixer or with a hand mixer.

Mix the sugar with the water in a saucepan and let it come to a rolling boil for 4–5 minutes, without stirring, until it turns into syrup. If it forms foam along the side of the pan, remove it with a spoon. If you have a candy thermometer, it should read 248 degrees F (120 degrees C). If not, you can do the ball test (see page 117, Coconut Balls).

Pour the boiling syrup in a thin stream into the half-whisked egg whites while the mixer runs at half speed. It is important that the sugar syrup hits right down in the meringue and not on the whisk. If the sugar syrup hits the whisk, throw the sugar syrup out to the side of the bowl.

Then, whip the meringue on full speed for 1 minute. It should still be warm.

Squeeze the water out of the soaked gelatin and add it to the meringue. Whisk until it is cooled. Sprinkle a little powdered sugar on a sheet of parchment paper and spread out the marshmallow mixture to approximately a ¾ in (1 ½ cm) thick layer. Sprinkle powdered sugar over the layer and let the mixture firm. It takes about 30 minutes. Cut the marshmallows in pieces and roll the pieces in powdered sugar. Sift off the powdered sugar before serving.

6 sheets of gelatin
2 egg whites (60 g)
1 tablespoon (20 g) heather
   honey
⅓ cup (1 dl) water
1 cup (200 g) sugar
a few drops of red food
   coloring, optional

Variations

Chocolate Marshmallows: Add 2 tablespoons (20 g) of finely chopped chocolate after the gelatin is whisked into the meringue.

Nut Marshmallows: Add ⅓ cup (50 g) chopped nuts to the marshmallow before it is spread out on the parchment paper.

Coconut Marshmallows: Add ⅓ cup (50 g) toasted shredded coconut to the marshmallow before it is spread out on the parchment paper.

Candied Flowers and Leaves

Candied flowers and leaves are great as a decoration for cakes and desserts. I candy by whipping together a little egg white and brushing lightly on both sides of the petal. After that, I sprinkle on finely ground sugar. You can either run the sugar in the food processor, or grind it in a mortar. Then you lay the flowers and leaves to dry on parchment paper at room temperature for approximately 12 hours.

Examples of Edible Flowers and Leaves

Violets, pansies, red clover, white clover, rose petals, carnation, wild and garden strawberry flowers, marigold, borage, black elderberry, cornflower, dandelion, mint, lemon balm.

NOTE! Flowers are not generally considered food, therefore spraying of pesticides is not taken into consideration. If you buy flowers for this use, you must therefore ensure that they are not sprayed.

Finished candied flowers and leaves can be stored several months in a jar at room temperature.

Chocolate

Everyone has a taste for chocolate. Milk or dark or white. I like to work with dark the most, because it has a high content of cocoa solids, and that's where the chocolate flavor is.

Dark chocolate consists of cocoa solids and sugar, while milk chocolate additionally contains dehydrated milk. When I work with milk chocolate, I use a version that contains 40% cocoa solids. Then, I think it still has a distinct chocolate flavor. Unfortunately, many chocolate manufacturers use less than 30% cocoa solids in milk chocolate, and then it doesn't taste so much like chocolate anymore.

Our intake of milk chocolate puts Norwegians in second place among the world's most chocolate-consuming people. Norway produces a lot of milk, and compared with other countries a lot of our dehydrated milk goes into chocolate production. We actually export dehydrated milk to the countries we later purchase finished milk chocolate from, like Belgium and France.

Therefore, chocolate is no longer produced in Norway, but in the Norwegian bakery, we have used chocolate since the 1800s, and obviously make it still.

❧ *Melting Chocolate*

Never expose chocolate to direct contact with the heat source. Melt it in a water bath (or microwave oven, see below). Use a boiler and a steel bowl that can hang inside the pot. The bowl shouldn't be so small that it falls into the pot. Fill the boiler with 1 in (3 cm) water, put it on the burner, and heat the water to the boiling point. The water should not boil, but be kept just below the boiling point.

Finely chop the chocolate and put it into the steel bowl. Put the bowl in the boiler and stir regularly until the chocolate is melted. This way, you have more control over the melting and can keep it from getting too warm. Be careful that steam or other moisture does not come in contact with the chocolate. Warm the chocolate to 113 degrees F (45 degrees C).

Melting in the microwave: Use half power. Finely chop the chocolate and melt it in short intervals of 20–30 seconds. Stir the chocolate between each interval.

❧ *Tempering Chocolate*

Should you use chocolate for something like dipping cookies, confections, and assorted chocolate garnishes, it is important that the chocolate goes through a process called tempering. In order to get a shiny, smooth chocolate that hardens quickly, one must be capable in the art of tempering. It is not difficult, just a little tedious. It is not too much of a problem if you don't always get it right the first time, because the chocolate can be melted and used again.

Whenever you temper chocolate, it is important to have a good thermometer that measures from 77–122 degrees F (25–50 degrees C). It is difficult to specify the amount of chocolate, but it is easier to get a successful result with a relatively big portion than a small one. Use a minimum of 15 oz (425 g). Whatever is left over can be saved and

tempered again on another occasion. It pays off to use a chocolate with a relatively high content of cocoa butter. Dark chocolate with less than 50% cocoa solids contains too little cocoa butter and doesn't really melt down. It gets viscous and is not suitable.

The tempering process is the same for dark, light, and white chocolate.

1. Melt the chocolate as explained above. When the chocolate reaches 113 degrees F (45 degrees C), pour ⅓ of it into another bowl. Put the bowl with the remaining ⅔ of the chocolate in a cold water bath, preferably with some ice cubes. The water should be in contact with the bowl. Stir the chocolate constantly with a spatula until the temperature is 80 degrees F (27 degrees C). When the temperature drops to 80 degrees F (27 degrees C), the chocolate will begin to get slightly thicker. Be careful so water does not get into the chocolate.

2. Remove the bowl from the cold water bath and dry the underside of the bowl. Stir in the ⅓ that is not cooled down. The temperature should then come up to 86–90 degrees F (30–32 degrees C). It is this temperature that is the "working temperature," and when it falls, you can warm it up again. I usually have a little melted chocolate at 113 degrees F (45 degrees C) that I add when the chocolate in the bowl begins to get cold and thicken. Make sure that the chocolate does not rise above 93 degrees F (34 degrees C). If that happens, you must start the process from the beginning again.

When the chocolate reaches the desired temperature, you can take a test to check if it is properly tempered: insert the tip of a knife into the chocolate and put the knife in the refrigerator for 30 seconds. If the chocolate is tempered correctly, it will begin to harden with an even color.

Blueberry Chocolates

The flavor of blueberry is round and mild. This flavor must be treated with care so it does not disappear. Therefore, when I make blueberry chocolates, I use sweet and mild milk chocolate. With that as a background, the delicate blueberry flavor clearly comes out.

Finely chop the chocolate. Run the blueberries in a blender.

Bring the blueberry purée and the corn syrup to a boil and pour it over the finely chopped milk chocolate. Stir until you get a smooth mixture. Start by stirring in the middle of the bowl in small circles with a spatula (if everything doesn't melt down, the bowl can be set in a water bath and heated gently while constantly stirring). The mixture can also be run into a smooth mixture with a hand mixer or in a food processor. Flavor with blueberry liqueur.

Cool the mixture to 93 degrees F (34 degrees C).

Stir in the softened butter. Pour the mixture into a pan with parchment paper so that it is ¼ in (½ cm) thick.

Set the mixture to cool overnight at 50–60 degrees F (12–16 degrees C). Remove the mixture from the pan and cut it into squares of 1 ¼ x ¾ in (3 x 2 cm) with a sharp knife. Heat the knife a little in warm water and dry it so it is easier to cut the chocolate.

Dip the squares in the tempered milk chocolate and put them on parchment paper. Then, decorate with dried blueberries (see page 79).

Place the chocolates in the refrigerator for 30 seconds until they begin to harden. Remove them and let them completely harden.

makes approximately
    50 pieces

½ cup (120 g) blueberries
10 oz (300 g)
    milk chocolate
1 teaspoon corn syrup
2 teaspoons (10 g) unsalted
    butter, softened
1 teaspoon blueberry li-
    queur

10 ½ oz (300 g) tempered
    milk chocolate for dipping
    (see page 137)

Chocolate Spots with Dried Berries

You make spots by piping chocolate rounds on a sheet of parchment paper. Then, you sprinkle on dried fruit and berries, nuts, and seeds. Everyone can make their mark on the chocolate by selecting what they like best. I've used dried strawberries and blueberries, and toasted pumpkin seeds. If you use nuts, kernels, or seeds, you should toast them first. This heat-treats the oil so that it releases the flavor and the result becomes richer in taste.

Preheat the oven to 350 degrees F (180 degrees C).

Toast the pumpkin seeds, and optional nuts, for about 10 minutes until they are golden brown.

Cool them.

Finely chop the chocolate, melt, and temper it (see page 137).

Put the chocolate in a piping bag with a ¼ in (½ cm) smooth tip and pipe spots the size of a silver dollar.

Decorate the top of the spots with dried berries and pumpkin seeds or chopped nuts. Set them to cool at 50–60 degrees F (12–16 degrees C).

makes approximately 50 pieces

1 cup (200 g) assorted dried berries, such as strawberries, blueberries, or raspberries (see page 79), and pumpkin seeds or nut kernels

1 lb 2 oz (500 g) dark chocolate or milk chocolate

Chocolate Cookies

These cookies are baked with brown sugar and dipped in milk chocolate. In addition, I have sprinkled on a little grated orange peel. It's been a long time since we discovered that crisp cookies with chocolate are fantastic. This is my twist on the classic hiking chocolate.

Wash the orange well in lukewarm water. Grate the peel (just the orange part) of the orange on a grater. Press the juice.

Cut the flour, baking powder, sugar, and butter in a bowl until crumbly, by hand or in a food processor.

Add the eggs and the orange juice and knead it into the dough, or quickly run the dough in a food processor.

Wrap the dough in plastic and let it rest for at least 1 hour in the refrigerator.

Preheat the oven to 320 degrees F (160 degrees C).

Roll the dough to an approximately ⅛ in (3 mm) thick sheet. Sprinkle the grated orange peel over the dough. Sprinkle on brown sugar for decoration and roll it lightly down into the dough. Cut cookies of approximately 1 ¼ x 4 in (3 x 10 cm). Place them on a baking sheet with parchment paper and bake them for 12–15 minutes until they are golden.

Cool.

Melt the chocolate (see page 137), and dip the cookies in it. Place them on parchment paper until they harden.

makes approximately
40 pieces

1 orange
3 cups (400 g) flour
½ tablespoon baking powder
1 cup (200 g) brown sugar
1 cup (200 g) salted butter, softened
2 eggs (100 g)
4 tablespoons brown sugar for decoration

7 oz (200 g) milk chocolate for dipping

Red Currant Chocolates

Tart and fresh red currants are perfect with sweet and rich chocolate. Milk chocolate is sweeter and fatter than dark chocolate and needs a sour component. I made these red currant chocolates for the first time for a Norwegian buffet at Hotel Fullerton in Singapore. I gave them a rough appearance that should fit with all of the images we have of Norway with the mountain landscape and fjords, forests, and fields.

Finely chop the chocolate. Run the red currants in a blender and strain. Measure it. You should have ⅓ cup (1 dl) red currant purée.

Boil the red currant purée and the corn syrup and pour it over the finely chopped milk chocolate. Stir until you get a smooth mixture. Start by stirring in the middle of the bowl in small circles with a spatula (if all of it doesn't melt down, the bowl can be put in a water bath and warmed carefully while constantly stirring). The mixture can also be run into a smooth mixture with a hand mixer or a food processor.

Cool the mixture to 93 degrees F (34 degrees C).

Stir in the softened butter. Pour the mixture into a pan with parchment paper so that it is ¼ in (½ cm) thick.

Set the mixture for cooling overnight at 50–60 degrees F (12–16 degrees C). Remove the mixture from the pan, and cut it into squares of 1 ¼ x ¾ in (3 x 2 cm) with a sharp knife. Heat the knife slightly in warm water and dry it, so it's easier to cut the chocolates.

Dip the squares in tempered dark chocolate and roll them in cocoa. Set them aside. When the chocolate has hardened, shake the chocolates in a sifter in order to get the excess cocoa off.

makes approximately 50 pieces

¾ cup (150 g) red currants
10 ½ oz (300 g) milk chocolate
1 teaspoon corn syrup
2 teaspoons (10 g) unsalted butter, softened

approximately 10 ½ oz (300 g) tempered dark chocolate (see page 137), for dipping
approximately ¾ cup (100 g) cocoa powder for decoration

Salt Caramel with Kviteseid Butter

The first time I had butter made with sour cream was at my grandmother's in Selbu. She had made butter "the old way," as she put it. This butter tasted better than regular butter. It was both sour and salty. The first time I made caramel with sour cream butter was in my grandmother's kitchen. Many years after, I've come to dip the caramel in chocolate and sprinkle on some salt flakes. The salt works like an extra flavor enhancer. The result was so good that I took the caramel chocolates along as the selection we won the Culinary Olympics with in 2008. It is also the most sold chocolate I have in my shop. It was impossible for a long time to obtain butter made with sour cream, but a few years back, Tine Dairy began to produce Kviteseid butter. This is the butter I use when I make my salted caramel chocolates.

Finely chop the milk chocolate. Put the sugar in a small boiler and heat it to caramel. Remove the boiler from the burner and add the butter. Stir until the butter is melted. Add the whipping cream, bring it all to a boil, and pour it over the finely chopped milk chocolate. Stir until you get a smooth mixture. Start with stirring in the middle of the bowl in small circles with a spatula (if everything doesn't melt down, the bowl can be set in a water bath and warmed carefully while constantly stirring). The mixture can also be run into a smooth mixture with a hand mixer or in a food processor.

Pour the mixture into a pan with parchment paper so that it's approximately ½ in (1 cm) thick.

Set the mixture overnight for cooling at 50–60 degrees F (12–16 degrees C). Take the batch out of the pan and cut squares of 1 ¼ x ¾ in (3 x 2 cm) with a sharp knife. Heat the knife a little in warm water and dry it so it's easier to cut the chocolates.

Dip the squares in tempered dark chocolate and set them on a sheet of parchment paper.

Decorate with a little Maldon salt.

Put the confections in the refrigerator for 1 minute until they begin to harden. Take them out and let them completely harden.

makes approximately
 40 pieces

¼ cup (50 g) sugar
3 tablespoons (50 g)
 Kviteseid butter
⅓ cup (1 dl) whipping cream
9 oz (250 g) milk
 chocolate

10 oz (300 g) tempered dark
 chocolate (see page 137),
 for dipping
some salt flakes for decoration (I prefer Maldon salt)

Porcini Mushroom Chocolates

During the Culinary Olympics in 2008, part of the assignment was to make five types of chocolates. Throughout the assignment, we wanted to present the best Norway has to offer, and we selected raspberry, rose hip, cloudberry, and pear. In addition, we wanted to challenge the judges by using something a little more unusual. After an extensive exploration of possible flavor combinations with chocolate, we landed on porcini mushroom. The porcini mushroom has a rich flavor that is not too prominent. The flavor should not characterize the chocolate, but eventually come forward a little as you chew, and create a roundness in the chocolate. The judges had a great appreciation for this special chocolate.

Run the porcini mushrooms into a fine powder in a food processor.

Bring the whipping cream to a boil with the porcini mushrooms. Remove the pan from the burner and put the lid on. Let the mixture soak for 15 minutes.

Finely chop the chocolate.

Bring the cream to a boil and pour it over the finely chopped chocolate. Stir until you get a smooth mixture. Blend the mixture with a hand blender or in a food processor.

Cool the mixture to 93 degrees F (34 degrees C).

Stir in the softened butter. Empty the mixture into a pan with parchment paper so that it's ¼ in (½ cm) thick.

Set the mixture to cool overnight at 50–60 degrees F (12–16 degrees C). Remove the batch from the pan and cut squares of approximately 1 ¼ x 1 ¼ in (3 x 3 cm) with a sharp knife. Heat the knife a little in warm water and dry it, so it's easier to cut the chocolates.

Dip the squares in tempered dark chocolate, and put them on a sheet of parchment paper. Place a little gold leaf on the tops of the chocolates, then place foil or a smooth surface such as plastic film over the gold leaf and use a brush to press it lightly onto the chocolate.

Set the chocolates in the refrigerator for 1 minute. Let them stand for 1 hour before you take the foil off. If the chocolate is well tempered, it gets completely smooth on the side that lay against the plastic.

makes approximately
 40 pieces

2 oz (50 g) dried porcini
 mushrooms
⅔ cup (1 ½ dl) whipping
 cream
10 oz (300 g) milk
 chocolate
2 teaspoons (10 g) unsalted
 butter, softened

approximately 10 oz
 (300 g) tempered dark
 chocolate (see page 137),
 for dipping
some gold leaf for decoration

Basic Recipes

Vanilla Cream

Split the vanilla bean and scrape out the seeds.

Put ¾ cup (2 dl) milk, the vanilla bean, seeds, whipping cream, and sugar in a saucepan (the saucepan should not be more than half full), mix it, and heat it to the boiling point.

Put the remaining milk and cornstarch in a bowl and lightly whisk together. Whisk the egg yolks into the milk and cornstarch mixture.

Gradually pour ⅔ of the heated liquid into the egg mixture while stirring with a whisk.

Then, pour the mixture back into the pan. Let the mixture come to a boil and simmer for 1 minute while constantly stirring in the bottom of the pan with a whisk (use a strong hand whisk), so that the cream doesn't burn.

Remove the vanilla bean after the cream has cooked. Pour the cream into a bowl. It is important that the cream is cooled quickly after it has boiled. Cover the cream with plastic and set it in the refrigerator.

1 vanilla bean
¾ cup + ¼ cup (2 dl + ½ dl) milk
⅓ cup (¾ dl) whipping cream
¼ cup (55 g) sugar
2 small egg yolks (30 g)
1 tablespoon + 1 teaspoon (20 g) cornstarch

Coffee Cream

The same as vanilla cream, but add 1 teaspoon (6 g) instant coffee to the milk after it has come to a boil.

Anise Cream

The same as vanilla cream, but replace the vanilla bean with 2 star anise.

Vanilla Butter Cream

Pour the vanilla cream into an electric mixer and beat until cooled, 75 degrees F (25 degrees C), with a beater.

Then add the softened butter and powdered sugar and beat on full speed until it's a smooth cream. The cream will look separated in the beginning, but will blend eventually. If the cream gets too liquid, it can be set in the refrigerator for a few minutes so that it begins to firm before it's whipped smooth again.

1 recipe for vanilla cream. Make vanilla cream, but don't chill it.
⅔ cup (150 g) unsalted butter, softened
¼ cup (30 g) powdered sugar

Coffee Butter Cream

Pour the cream in an electric mixer and beat until cooled, 75 degrees F (25 degrees C), with a beater.

Then add the softened butter and powdered sugar and whip on full speed until it becomes a smooth cream. The cream will look separated in the beginning, but will blend eventually. If the cream gets too liquid, it can be put in the refrigerator for a few minutes so that it begins to firm before it's whipped smooth again.

1 recipe for coffee cream. Make vanilla cream, but don't chill it.
⅔ cup (150 g) unsalted butter, softened
¼ cup (30 g) powdered sugar

Easy Vanilla Cream

Make vanilla cream, but don't chill it. Soak the gelatin in cold water for about 5 minutes

Squeeze the water out of the gelatin and stir it into the heated vanilla cream.

Cool.

Whip the whipping cream. Stir the vanilla cream until smooth and fold it into the whipped cream.

1 recipe for vanilla cream
2 sheets of gelatin
1 ½ cups (4 dl) whipping cream

Oxalis Cream

Make vanilla cream, but don't chill it. Soak the gelatin in cold water for about 5 minutes.

Squeeze the water out of the gelatin and stir it into the heated vanilla cream.

Cool.

Put the vanilla cream in a food processor together with the oxalis leaves, and run it so that the oxalis gets finely chopped and the cream is green.

Whip the whipping cream. Stir the vanilla cream until smooth and fold it into the whipped cream.

1 recipe for vanilla cream
2 sheets of gelatin
¾ cup (2 dl) oxalis leaves
1 ½ cups (4 dl) whipping cream

Basic Sponge Cake

Preheat the oven to 350 degrees F (180 degrees C).

Beat the eggs and sugar in an electric mixer until frothy.

Sift the flour and fold it into the egg mixture with a spatula.

Cover a baking sheet with greased parchment paper. Spread the batter out on the parchment paper to approximately a ½ in (1 cm) thick layer.

Bake the cake in the middle of the oven for 15 minutes until it is golden. Try to lift up the edge of the cake from the paper. If the parchment paper releases, the cake is done.

Cool.

makes 1 baking sheet,
**   12 x 10 in (30 x 25 cm)**

8 eggs (400 g)
1 cup (200 g) sugar
1 ⅛ cups (150 g) flour

Basic Tart Crust

Cut the flour, powdered sugar, and butter in a bowl until crumbly, by hand or in a food processor.

Add the egg and knead it until it forms a dough, or quickly blend the dough in a food processor.

Wrap the dough in plastic and let it rest at least 2 hours in the refrigerator. If there's dough left over, it can be wrapped in plastic and kept for up to 3 weeks in the freezer.

yields 3 cups (650 g) dough

2 ¼ cups (300 g) flour
14 tablespoons (200 g) cold
**   unsalted butter in ¾ in**
**   (2 cm) cubes**
¾ cup (100 g) powdered
**   sugar**
1 egg

Basic Carrot Cake

Preheat the oven to 350 degrees F (180 degrees C).

Wash and peel the carrots. Grate them finely on a grater. Beat the eggs and sugar in a food processor. Add the oil in a thin stream while the mixer beats half speed. Fold the carrot into the egg mixture with a spatula. Sift in the flour and baking powder, and fold it with a spatula. Fold in the raisins toward the end.

Cover a baking sheet with parchment paper. Spread the cake batter in approximately a ½ in (1 cm) thick layer on the parchment paper with a spatula.

Bake the cake in the middle of the oven until golden, approximately 20 minutes. Try to lift up a corner of the cake. If the parchment paper releases, the cake is done. Turn the cake upside down on a piece of parchment paper that is sprinkled with sugar, and pull off the parchment paper the cake is baked on. Baked cakes can be wrapped in plastic and kept up to 1 month in the freezer.

makes 1 baking sheet, 12 x 10 in (30 x 25 cm)

2 ½ medium-sized carrots (300 g) carrot
3 eggs (150 g)
1 cup (200 g) sugar
1 cup (2 ½ dl) soy oil
1 ¼ cups (170 g) flour
1 ½ teaspoons baking powder
½ cup (75 g) raisins

Basic Almond Cake

Preheat the oven to 350 degrees F (180 degrees C).

Run the almonds and powdered sugar into fine flour in a food processor. Beat the egg white and sugar into a stiff meringue. Fold the almond mixture into the meringue with a spatula.

Line a baking sheet with parchment paper and spread the batter out to an approximately ½ in (1 cm) thick layer. Bake the cake in the middle of the oven for approximately 15 minutes. Try to lift up a corner of the cake. If the parchment paper releases, the cake is done.

1 ¼ cups (150 g) almonds
¾ cup (100 g) powdered sugar
4 egg whites (120 g)
¼ cup (50 g) sugar

Crumbled Sweet Rusks

Preheat the oven to 335 degrees F (170 degrees C).

Mix all the ingredients well in a bowl. Crumble the dough over a baking sheet lined with parchment paper. Bake until golden.

Cool.

If the pieces are big, you can crumble them a little more with your hands.

¾ cup (100 g) flour

7 tablespoons (100 g) salted butter, softened

¾ cup (100 g) powdered sugar

¾ cup (100 g) ground almonds

½ teaspoon ground cardamom

Caramelized Bread

Cut the crusts off the bread and cut the bread in strips or cubes.

Melt the butter in a frying pan. Sprinkle the bread with powdered sugar and fry it in butter until the powdered sugar is lightly caramelized.

The bread can also be crushed into crumbs after it has been cooled.

2 slices of bread

2 tablespoons butter

3 tablespoons powdered sugar

Dark Chocolate Glaze

Finely chop the chocolate and melt it in a water bath (see page 137 for correct melting of chocolate).

Bring the sugar, corn syrup, and ⅔ cup (1 ½ dl) whipping cream to a boil. Pour the cream in a thin stream down into the chocolate while you stir in small circles with a spatula, so that it forms an emulsion between chocolate and cream. It is important not to use a whisk, because that makes air bubbles in the glaze. If you use a spatula or ladle, you get a smooth and glossy glaze. Stir in ¼ cup (½ dl) cold cream toward the end. It makes the glaze glossier.

This glaze can be kept in the freezer for up to 1 month. When it's used again, it should be carefully thawed and warmed in a water bath on the burner or in the microwave in short intervals.

7 oz (200 g) dark chocolate
   with 60% cocoa solids
⅔ + ¼ cup (1 ½ + ½ dl)
   whipping cream
¼ cup (50 g) sugar
1 ½ tablespoons (25 g)
   corn syrup or honey

Library of Congress Cataloging-in-Publication Data is available on file.

ISBN: 978-1-5107-2203-3
EISBN: 978-1-62873-309-9

Printed in China

Conversion Charts

METRIC AND IMPERIAL CONVERSIONS
(These conversions are rounded for convenience)

Ingredient	Cups/Tablespoons/Teaspoons	Ounces	Grams/Milliliters
Butter	1 cup = 16 tablespoons = 2 sticks	8 ounces	230 grams
Cheese, shredded	1 cup	4 ounces	110 grams
Cream cheese	1 tablespoon	0.5 ounce	14.5 grams
Cornstarch	1 tablespoon	0.3 ounce	8 grams
Flour, all-purpose	1 cup/1 tablespoon	4.5 ounces/0.3 ounce	125 grams/8 grams
Flour, whole wheat	1 cup	4 ounces	120 grams
Fruit, dried	1 cup	4 ounces	120 grams
Fruits or veggies, chopped	1 cup	5 to 7 ounces	145 to 200 grams
Fruits or veggies, puréed	1 cup	8.5 ounces	245 grams
Honey, maple syrup, or corn syrup	1 tablespoon	.75 ounce	20 grams
Liquids: cream, milk, water, or juice	1 cup	8 fluid ounces	240 milliliters
Oats	1 cup	5.5 ounces	150 grams
Salt	1 teaspoon	0.2 ounce	6 grams
Spices: cinnamon, cloves, ginger, or nutmeg (ground)	1 teaspoon	0.2 ounce	5 milliliters
Sugar, brown, firmly packed	1 cup	7 ounces	200 grams
Sugar, white	1 cup/1 tablespoon	7 ounces/0.5 ounce	200 grams/12.5 grams
Vanilla extract	1 teaspoon	0.2 ounce	4 grams

OVEN TEMPERATURES

Fahrenheit	Celsius	Gas Mark
225°	110°	$1/4$
250°	120°	$1/2$
275°	140°	1
300°	150°	2
325°	160°	3
350°	180°	4
375°	190°	5
400°	200°	6
425°	220°	7
450°	230°	8